THE
AUTONOMOUS MAN

By the Same Author:
Lonely God, Lonely Man

THE
AUTONOMOUS MAN

An Essay in Personal Identity and Integrity

DEAN TURNER

THE BETHANY PRESS

ST. LOUIS, MISSOURI

© *1970 by The Bethany Press*

Library of Congress Catalog Card Number: 71-105052

Scripture quotations, unless otherwise noted,
are from the *Revised Standard Version of the Bible,*
copyrighted 1946 and 1952 by the
Division of Christian Education, National
Council of Churches of Christ in the United
States of America, and used by permission.

Distributed by The G. R. Welch Company, Toronto, Ontario, Canada.
Other foreign distribution by Feffer and Simons, Inc., New York, New York.

MANUFACTURED IN THE UNITED STATES OF AMERICA

For Nancy-bo,
My Woman,
My Wife,
Who has taught me the meaning of
"My cup runneth over."

Contents

Introduction

CONSIDERING the mountains of books already written on the subject of integrity, one might wonder if there remains any possibility of genuinely new contributions. I certainly feel that one should avoid writing in this field unless he is convinced that he has some new ideas, or at least a fresh way of presenting some old ones to accomplish something not heretofore accomplished. I think we should at the beginning take note of one fact: there are still untold numbers of persons in our society who are so deprived of integrity that they are emotionally, intellectually, and morally sick. In fact, this is true in almost every culture in the world. I do not know offhand of any culture that is characterized by a preponderance of high individual integrity in most of its members. There surely must be some explanation for this. In this book I purport to offer an explanation; also, I want to present a new philosophy of personal autonomy to try to help alleviate our sad human situation.

I am convinced that the most esteemed writers dealing with this problem have failed to come up with a basically adequate palliative for humanity's spiritual sickness. As anyone knows who has read the myriad scholarly books attempting to diagnose the problem, this sickness certainly has been adequately *described*. The trouble is that the psychologists and sociologists have satisfied themselves basically with nothing more than a description of what is wrong. For example, William H. Whyte, in his *Organization Man,* brilliantly and diligently portrays a true picture of what has happened to a society that has sickened itself trying to live by the false principles of the "Social Ethic." Too many Americans have tried to honor the traditional spirit of individualism while also honoring the Social Ethic, and the twain simply can never unite. Whyte's description of the failure of the Social Ethic to unite humanity in positive ways is valid and trenchantly interesting. However, we need more than a merely true and exciting description of our patterns of social conformity that are unhealthy.

In his *Lonely Crowd,* David Riesman cleverly unveils the social pressures which he thinks have browbeaten the average American into compromising his selfhood, his sense of individual worth, and his independence. Riesman's book was published over a decade ago, but it is still one of the most widely read and appreciated criticisms of the society of our time. Nevertheless, the genius of Riesman's power for sociological analysis does not keep him from being a typical sociologist: he seems to be fascinated by analysis and description of social patterns and conditions, but offers no real palliative, no clear philosophy of personal autonomy. He presents no set of principles upon which the individual can peg his daily life and preserve his identity and integrity. We need more than merely to describe and classify conformists and their social pressures. Riesman's book includes only one chapter on autonomy. He expresses a desire and hope that the masses of Americans will have a change of mind and heart, that we will decide to become more real and autonomous persons. But just to hope certainly is not enough. Riesman does not explain what autonomy is. He offers his readers no set of principles for self-direction, self-management, or self-evaluation. Basically, he confines himself to diagnosing symptoms of character sickness, but prescribes no remedy. Nor does he clearly contrast the characteristics of the unhealthy conformist with those of the autonomous or healthy man.

Popular nonprofessional social critics seem to offer no more direction than do the sociologists and career psychologists. For example, England's Colin Wilson is neither a professional sociologist, nor psychologist, nor philosopher. However, he is an unusually original and imaginative writer, and sometimes a very lucid social critic. In his *Age of Defeat,* he accuses the average American and Englishman of having an "insignificanse neurosis," a deflated ego, a basic spiritual cowardice, an addiction to arbitrary norms, etc. *Age of Defeat* reads like an exciting novel. Wilson's analysis of human character weaknesses is insightful, unsparing, and sharpens the reader's understanding of some of his own motives and negative nature. His descriptions of the "anti-hero complex," the "ordinary-chap cult," and the "insignificanse neurosis" are ingenious and imaginative generalizations. Also, they are truthful enough to arouse the reader to feel more obsession for achieving personal greatness in his own life. Moreover, Wilson manages to describe our cultural weaknesses trenchantly, yet with a basic humility in his analysis and an attitude of sympathy.

Even so, his critical concern with the problems of autonomy generally is merely descriptive and largely negative. Like so many others, he complains against conformity while pleading for integrity. But if the reader is looking for a philosophy and psychology of integrity *en positivo,* he cannot find it in Wilson, any more than in Whyte or in Riesman. Wilson announces himself as an existentialist and seems to show no awareness that we need a philosophy of autonomy consisting of a set of definite principles. I contend that all humanity needs such a philosophy, a set of objectively valid principles that every individual must peg his daily life on if his individualism is to be altruistic and rational. No individualism can survive that ultimately is self-enveloped or merely subjective and capricious or whimsical. Wilson takes note of this fact several times in his book. He emphasizes the need for self-discipline, circumspection, and serious self-study. Yet, he terminates his short treatment of autonomy with the stance of an existentialist, offering the reader no clear principles that are valid for all human beings in common.

I strenuously object to the doctrine that individual ethics must ultimately be merely subjective and personal. If there are no principles of ethical autonomy that are objectively valid for all, then there can be no objectively valid distinction between altruistic individualism and individualism that is selfish. Nor can there be any meaningful distinction between ir-rational individualism and morality that is rational.

The psychology shelves in our libraries are lined with books treating of integrity and identity. In his *Meaning of Anxiety,* Rollo May exposes those reductionistic psychologies that refuse to accept a human being as a spirit, an *agent,* a concrete individual entity. We live in an age of phenomenological psychologies which deny that a man is a *soul,* a being *sui generis.* Discarding the soul, these psychologies reduce man to a social and biological *product* and deny that he is a free agent. Man is left without any explanation for his memory, continuity of consciousness, and unity of personality. A viable ethic of personal autonomy cannot possibly be built upon a soulless psychology, and May explains some of the reasons why. The in-sightfulness of his agent-psychology exceeds even Paul Tillich's in *Courage to Be.* Both men look upon man as a spiritual agent, a being who is logically and existentially distinct from other persons and things around him. Thus, they lay objec-tive grounds for an ethic of autonomy and present a clear rationale of individual responsibility and freedom. I especially profited from their explanations of the origin of anxiety out of freedom, of the impossibility of escaping from anxiety in life. Unlike the psychologists of other schools, Tillich and May obligate the individual with full responsibility for his free decisions, his virtues and sins. Nevertheless, they too end up with basically a merely descriptive psychology, and past the rationale of freedom they simply do not move toward specific principles of an objective ethic of autonomy.

Among professional philosophers, I have had the same dif-ficulty in finding a principled approach to the philosophy of autonomy. It has been said that sociologists generally are fascinated by descriptions, while philosophers are obsessed with speculations and explanations. I have found much cause to doubt this. In fact, these days just the opposite seems to be the truth about the philosophers. For if I accurately assess the history of thought, there has been no age to equal our own in its penchant for nit-picking analysis, its enjoyment in splitting infinitely small academic hairs, its satisfaction with generally destructive and negative criticism. I do, of course, know philosophers who are creative, speculative, and who strive to interpret life in terms of positive values, facts, and principles, instead of negations. But in truth, I know many more professional philosophers (teachers in the schools) who seem to thrive on negation, critical dissection, and a preoccupation with the kind of semantical and linguistic analysis that is largely useless and academic. A graduate student of mine once said, "Never before has there been a time endowed with so many learned thinkers." I myself question whether there has ever been a time when more "thinkers" have so greatly enjoyed "straining out a gnat and swallowing a camel."

The purpose of philosophy should be to discover and interpret facts, ideas, and principles with which we can expand our being. A philosophy is great only to the extent that it enriches our identity, our social relations, and gives us fulfilling and challenging adventures in life. There certainly are many great philosophers who have demonstrated an acute awareness of this fact. It is not my purpose to raise doubt in this regard, nor to spread cynicism.

I should call witness, for example, to the fiery spirit of individualism in Sören Kierkegaard's *Purity of Heart Is to Will One Thing*. What man, other than Jesus (to whom Kierkegaard devoted his life), has more clearly exemplified the affirmation of the value of the individual human spirit? In Kierkegaard, we find the theory of autonomy matched with consistent daily practice—in the willingness to suffer social insolvency to any extent, in behalf of being true to himself, to his individual needs and convictions. One's personal power is continuously strengthened as he reads the pages of the Great Dane's thought and life. No psychologist or philosopher before or after Kierkegaard has seen more clearly into the realities of the human struggle for self-meaning and self-importance. In reading Kierkegaard, one realizes the necessity to accept anxiety, to accept the responsibility and freedom of being human, or to live with it inescapably whether one accepts it or not.

Reading *Sickness unto Death,* one explores with Kierkegaard all the avenues of escape from the responsibility of facing oneself, others, and God. One comes to see clearly that *there can be no escape.* Even in self-destruction, or in the severest form of self-deception, there can be no escape. In part, the individual may choose to make his own essences. He may choose to exist either authentically or inauthentically. But however he chooses, he must pay a price for his choice. Authentic existence is painfully demanding. One exists authentically when he acts responsibly and exhausts his possibilities for self-fulfillment. He is inauthentic insofar as he negates these possibilities, or ignores or abuses them. The authentic man pays for his existence in the pains of his self-struggle and self-discipline. He must accept within himself the pain of effort in conquering his tendencies to inertia, and to escape. Also, he must pay with anxiety when he seeks beauty, truth, and goodness for their own sake and finds that society may hate these things and not understand them. He may be pressured to submit to people's ignorant will, but refuse to do it. Thus, he must pay if society rejects him, mocks him, tries to break him, or simply leaves him lonely. He must pay in separation, solitariness, and sadness. But of course, he is free; he may choose to submit to society's will even when he believes it most wrong. He then must pay with the anxiety of sin. This is the feeling of guilt which plagues him even when he represses it from his consciousness and attempts to justify it through that strange human capacity of believing one's own lies. Inauthenticity stalks the deceiver insofar as he would hide from himself, for no one can ever *completely* hide from himself; the deceiver cannot undo the fact that he is a split self, a false and disjointed being. And certainly, he can never hide from God.

I know of no philosopher or psychologist who offers more insight into the problems of autonomy than Kierkegaard. Concerning the price one must pay for authentic existence, I know of no one who has added to his description of the frustrations, pains, and fears that might plague the person who chooses to be real. Most certainly, I know of nothing I myself could add. Were I to enumerate the scars on my own body, the valleys of pain in my own past, the mountains of frustration and anxiety, I could not add, in principle, to the truth that one can find in studying the mind of this great man.

Nevertheless, I have a purpose in writing this book, and it is to do what Kierkegaard and all others (to my knowledge) dealing with the problems of autonomy have failed to do. Namely, I intend to go beyond the analysis of failure and the description of agonies to the construction of a positive and rational philosophy of autonomy. I intend to delineate and explain a set of principles that all of us must live by in order to exist as authentic individuals. Kierkegaard did not provide these principles. The exploration of the agonies is of very great value, but it is not enough. Rich as they are in depth psychology, Kierkegaard's works never produce an objective ethic, a set of principles which every person must live by if he is not to founder in a false individualism.

I must make a similar criticism of other philosophers of world renown for their contributions to the subject. For example, there are the European existentialists whose talk about "authentic" and "inauthentic" existence has amounted to literally thousands of pages: Gabriel Marcel, Martin Heidegger, Karl Jaspers, and Jean-Paul Sartre. Of another philosophical school (and known worldwide for his own peculiar style of individualism) is the redoubtable Bertrand Russell, an English atheist who has written on the subject no less colorfully than he is known to have acted. While honoring the worthwhile contributions Russell has made, I must include him in the list of failures, if what we are seeking is an ethic of autonomy that has objective validity. Russell's moral theory is simply suicidal: he categorically renounces the freedom of the will to choose between alternative possibilities for action at any given time. Furthermore, he reduces all morality, in theory, down to mere subjectivity, i.e., to matters of individual or personal *taste*.

In numerous writings, the French atheist Sartre speaks recurrently of the "authentic" man versus the "inauthentic" man, just as does Martin Heidegger (the notable German atheist) in *Being and Time*. I should say that both of these men fail for fundamentally the same reason that Mr. Russell

fails: they undermine all objective bases for ethics by con-
tending that everyone must make his own truths and values,
and that this is as far as truth and value can go. If this were
the case (that there are no objectively valid moral principles
that all of us *ought* to know and live by), an intelligible
philosophy of autonomy would be neither theoretically nor
practically possible. If there were no objective laws of rationality (i.e., if rationality and irrationality were merely subjective), then no individual would be guilty of irrational reasoning unless he believed it or admitted it. But this is utter
nonsense, for it should be obvious that no person has to be
aware of his contradictions in order to be contradictory in
his reasoning. In truth, if a man has contradictions in his reasoning, then his reasoning is illogical whether he knows it
or not, or admits it or not. Sartre's renunciation of objectively
valid laws of logic makes a meaningful distinction between
rational and irrational individualism impossible. In theory,
he also renounces objectively real moral laws and values.
Consequently, he ultimately abolishes any meaningful distinction between (1) what an individual *desires* to do, or does
do, and (2) what he *ought* to do, or has a moral obligation to
do. In renouncing the eternal verities that bind men with objective responsibility, atheism does the philosophy of morality an
inglorious violence. For ultimately, Sartre's "existential man"
and Russell's "chance man" (who is merely an "accidental
collocation of atoms") must feel that they live in a purely
happenstance world where they are bound by no definite intellectual and moral necessities whatever. Besides, atheism's
ultimate despairfulness is no attitude out of which one could
expect any sound ethic of autonomy ever to arise. No ethic
of individualism can do justice to us if it takes us out of our
context with the infinite and the eternal. No theory is legitimate that reduces the importance of a human life. We should
settle only for an ethic that uplifts man, never for one that
diminishes or downgrades him. Certainly no ethic is worthwhile that invites us to gloom (or justifies gloom) by saying
that we are doomed to return to that meaningless nothingness
out of which all of us have arisen accidentally and absurdly.

The atheists affront my experience of human worth. They mock the reality of my love. Did I come into the world to taste the sacred sweetness, the infinite beauty of love, only to be robbed of its meaning by a cold grave? Sartre and Russell would look down on me in the casket. They would say: In the end, the human spirit has the same destiny as the worm. You once existed, and you knew beauty, joy, and love. But now, you are *nothing*. You are nothing but a decomposing, stinking corpse. You are forever and ever, *nothing*.

I emphatically renounce this philosophy.

The atheistic relativists have despaired, and in their despair they have denied that what I am attempting to achieve in this book is possible. The religious relativists also have despaired, for they have denigrated God's gift of reason to man; they have defined faith as something totally blind in the utter darkness. No less than the nihilists, the religious relativists have denied the possibility of a set of objectively valid moral principles which can enlighten our lives. In his popular *Situation Ethics,* Bishop Joseph Fletcher argues for moral relativism with the passion of a dogmatist. After establishing a singular absolute of his own (that we must always act to serve God, through love), Fletcher denies that other principles of morality are feasible or possible. He thus leaves love so subject to subjectivism that one can only lament his radical failure to develop an ethic of autonomy. Unmistakably, Fletcher implies that any attempt to construct such an ethic can be only labor in vain.

In this book, I set forth to challenge these negative views. I believe that a principled ethic of autonomy not only is possible but is direly needed. Indeed, the knowledge and practice of these principles in love is all that can save humanity. Admittedly, I take upon myself an ambitious task. But then, what better excuse can one have for writing a new book?

PART ONE

The Nihilist
Ethic

1.

Reality: Something
That Never Is

IT IS perhaps unmanly to begin a first chapter with an apologia. I begin this one well aware of the fact that a discussion of relativism is not a logical necessity in the development of my philosophy. In Part Two, I shall present six ethical principles by which I contend everyone must live if he is to be an altruistic and rational individualist. I believe there can be no individual in any culture, or in any age, who can ignore or abuse these principles without therein being the loser and paying a high price. An objectively valid ethic is one that both the individual and society can most benefit from if everyone knows the principles and puts them into practice. Any individualism that is insensitive to the needs and rights of others must be detrimental and false. The individualism of selfish and irrational persons is self-impeding, if not actually self-destructive, simply because it breeds enemies instead of friends, and enemies can never fulfill one's life as much as friends. Friendliness and love should be our basic purposes in life. Friendly human relations offer all of us values and meanings which feelings of enmity simply can never produce.

True individualism acknowledges two different kinds of legitimate authority. One is the *self-authority* of the individual who has in his nature private or unique traits and needs which are not shared by society. No one's individualism is mature if he does not demand the right to be honored in his natural uniqueness and differences. One must recognize and fulfill these needs in himself, or else he will neglect and falsify his own nature out of conformity to society or to his own weaknesses. The other legitimate authority is *social*. This authority rests in the right of the social body to demand that individuals respect the nature and needs that all human beings have in common. Any individualism is false that does not honor in others the same needs and rights which it demands be honored in itself.

The doctrine of relativism, advocated by Fletcher in his "Situation Ethic," leaves all human rights and duties undefined. Bishop Fletcher refuses to state clear principles of authority whereby both the individual and society can demand protection from the injustices of each other. I accept his love principle (which he reverently attributes to the teachings of Jesus), and I shall incorporate it in the ethics of this book. However, it seems totally impractical and unrealistic to assume, as Fletcher does, that in our complex society we can relate successfully with one another on the basis of only one moral principle. Since his doctrine is very popular in current thinking, and since I regard it as false, I must concede that a philosophy of moral autonomy cannot be treated in full scope without a consideration of the relativist theory of human relations. This is not a logical necessity, for a sound ethical philosophy certainly can stand on its own. However, it is a practical necessity simply because of the widespread influence of the relativist doctrine.

Bishop Fletcher calls himself a pragmatist, and it is obvious that his widely read book has succeeded in converting thousands of readers into moral relativists. In the chapters on autonomy, I shall attempt to show that each of the principles I advance is grounded in objective reality, that the entire ethic has a validity transcending the relative subjectivity of mere personal opinion. If an ethic is objectively valid, then it is true whether any particular individual is aware or ignorant of it, whether or not he chooses to live by it, and whether or not he cares about it. I believe that Fletcher, and the great army of supporters he finds in pragmatism, cannot refute any of these principles without trampling on logic and the thousands of years of humanity's experience with moral values. I shall attempt to show that no one can refute these principles without cutting his own throat. These principles have a cogency that is rooted in the grounds of reality. They should be self-evident to any person who opens his mind and heart to both his own needs and those of others. If the relativism upon which Fletcher bases his "ethic" is correct, there can be no philosophy of morality with any compelling logical or factual validity. If the relativist doctrine of human relations is true, then even his love principle (which he takes as an absolute) must also turn out to be merely arbitrary and subjective. Although the principles of autonomy can stand on their own right (relativism allows nothing to stand on its own), I can strengthen my own case by delineating and refuting the tenets of relativism for any readers not familiar with them—and this could well include even some of the professional pragmatists. In theory, many of my colleagues object to any form of indoctrination or direct counseling. Yet in practice, their own classes often are propaganda courses in relativism, in which they direct continuous and concerted attacks upon realism, idealism, and any other doctrine which holds that we can have some certain knowledge of objective reality. That many pragmatists do not examine or understand the basic tenets of their own doctrine is intellectually amusing but morally disturbing. That many preach against indoctrination, while so enthusiastically practicing it themselves, plainly is hypocritical.

In this book, let there be no pretension to hide it: I claim to deal in objective truths and should like to see all humanity live by my ethic of autonomy. Insofar as pragmatism, in theory, would make the truths of this ethic impossible, I believe that I should list its tenets (as the pragmatists themselves have stated them), then attempt to refute them critically. The criticisms will be my own, along with a few that are common and borrowed from my colleagues. Certainly, the tenets that I attack will be presented exactly as I have found them stated in the literature of the leading pragmatists, namely, John Dewey, William James, Sidney Hook, Charles Frankel, William O. Stanley, Boyd H. Bode, Donald Arnstine, Frederick Neff, Earl

C. Cunningham, Lawrence G. Thomas, Theodore Brameld, and William Kilpatrick, to mention only a few.

The fundamental principles of pragmatism are:

1. The essence of reality is change; everything is constantly changing.
2. All values and truths are temporary, individual, and relative.
3. All judgments are arbitrary, fallible, and uncertain.
4. All truths are man-made.
5. The only knowledge which can be considered legitimate is that which can be scientifically demonstrated or publicly verified.
6. The criterion of truth is agreement among scientific observers.
7. There are no a priori truths (i.e., universal truths that are self-evident, grounded in reality and pure reason, and not in need of proof).
8. An idea is true if it works, if it brings satisfaction to whoever is attempting to solve a problem.
9. There are no intrinsic values or truths; no proposition is inherently true or false, and no thing (idea, object, person, etc.) has value in and of itself. Something is true or valuable only if it has satisfactory consequences when it is used, put into practice, and holds up under experimental testing.
10. All conclusions should be tentative.
11. Reality is experience; experience is reality.
12. Reality is a pure continuum; the world is one whole, and nature is *one* process.

If it could be shown that the above principles were true, then I should readily acknowledge that any viable philosophy of morality would be impossible. Indeed, I should be compelled to conclude that philosophy itself is impossible if its aim is to accrue *abiding* facts, principles, and values by which a person can wisely direct his life. There have been many piercing criticisms of pragmatism, all of which seem to add up to one chief objection, namely, that if this doctrine were true, any form of definite knowledge would be impossible. If pragmatism were true, the proper thing to do would be to abandon philosophy altogether. I agree with this, for it seems quite evident that all the principles of pragmatism undermine their own validity. The whole doctrine revolves in a vicious circle around obliquities, ambiguities, and *non sequiturs*. I once heard a psychiatrist declare that "pragmatists are inevitably nihilists, for while they renounce any possibility of real knowledge of the world, they at the same time claim to possess objectivity and to pursue truth responsibly. They suffer from an intellectual schizophrenia, which arises from their use of reason to destroy reason, truth to deny truth, and knowledge to universalize doubt."

I agree with this, and clap; for I have seen one pragmatist after another try glibly to persuade me with paralogisms (the use of valid principles of logic to deny the very validity of the selfsame principles). While studying at a pragmatist-dominated graduate school, I rarely was permitted to express really dissenting opinions even in the "seminars." Pragmatism often applauds itself for its open-mindedness, flexibility, and devotion to free discussion through democratic procedures. Thus, it is curious that not once in graduate school did I have a pragmatist professor who was tolerant of discussion. Yet all the while, these professors were attacking the realists and idealists for being "undemocratic" and "imposing their values on others."

The first tenet of pragmatism, that *everything constantly changes,* logically tears the floor out from under the entire doctrine. If everything were constantly changing, then no reality could abide, not even for a moment. There could be no essences, facts, values, meanings, ideas, objects, principles, or anything else, for the simple reason that no reality could remain itself, unchanged, long enough even to *be* what it *is*. According to pragmatism, there is no *being*, and there are no *beings*, in reality ever. Although the pragmatist insists that some things change faster or slower than other things, the assumption is ontologically meaningless; for how, one may ask, can speed of change make any logical difference if nothing in reality ever *is* what it *is*? This should be obvious: if nothing could remain itself, neither for a long nor for a short period of time, then no one could say that its nature was constantly changing, simply because it could never have any definite nature to change.

In his *Quest for Being,* pragmatist Sidney Hook appears to deny that reality contains any beings whatever. He reduces everything substantial and abiding down to a mere process of becoming and unbecoming. If I read him correctly, he leaves nothing in the universe which we can meaningfully say "exists." It may well be that I have misunderstood Hook. To be sure, I do not claim to understand him, if this means finding any real clarity in his thinking. He continuously employs the verb "to be" in all its forms and refers to the existence of something in every sentence he writes. There is not a single statement in any of his books in which he does not presuppose the *existence* of something. Yet, he says, "The question is . . . whether the word 'being' has *any* meaning in a philosophical context, and by a philosophical context I mean any activity which inquires into the logic and the *procedures* by which knowledge is built up and described."[1] It appears to me that Hook is guilty of unconsciously presupposing the existence of many truths and realities that he consciously denies have "*any* philosophical meaning." Either I am not following him correctly here, or else I do follow him, and I end up in a universe which has no "philosophically meaningful" beings at all—and I am worse off than ever.

If there were no abiding realities, there could be no fixities or structures in the world, and no permanency of meanings. Therefore, intelligible communication or thought of any kind would be impossible. What is more, there could be no enduring values or truths whatever, and this is an intolerable notion to those of us who want to conserve the meanings and values in our knowledge and love. Also, a pointless mockery is made of common sense—that reality is forever becoming and unbecoming, yet never succeeds in producing any *beings* who are conscious of *that which is* becoming *what.* If our knowledge of the beings we find in the world were a mere illusion, there could be no existing persons even to talk about becoming and unbecoming. The truth is that we can never talk meaningfully of becoming or unbecoming unless we also at the same time refer to some being.

For example, *I* am becoming disillusioned by many philosophers. I *exist*. I have *being*. I *am*. I am not just becoming human; I *am* human. I am not just becoming Dean Turner; I *am* Dean Turner. My identity *abides*. I shall not awaken tomorrow and discover that I am Bertha Rainmaker, another person who is an entirely different agent. No, I shall awaken as Dean Turner, I who have been I all the days of my life. I shall awaken in contact with my background of history, with a memory of my life, of my own past experiences. I must admit that my conscious experiences are a stream of ever-changing thoughts, moods, ideas, images, and sundry mental states. But it is also true that I transcend these states, that I am aware of the change, the dynamic and cumulative nature of my experience of life. Nevertheless, I the agent *in* whom these experiences occur and *to* whom they belong remain the same agent. I am not in the habit of mistaking myself for another; and I have never, nor shall I ever, become another. Of course my own identity will expand. But I shall remain I. Not all the pragmatists on earth can argue the fact that I am an abiding agent, with some abiding knowledge, purposes, and values that have become a permanent part of my self. I not only *am* a human being; I have *been* (remained) a human being for forty-two years, despite the continuous changes that have expanded my identity.

If everything constantly changed, it would be impossible for anybody to know this as a fact, for the simple reason that nobody's capacity to know it could possibly abide. Or, if somebody had an abiding capacity to know it, then it would be a false assumption that there can be no abiding capacities—which, anyway you look at it, would undermine the validity of the pragmatist's first tenet.

The members of this school would be hard put to prove their basic premise. How, for example, could they prove that the *past* changes or unbecomes? Realistically speaking, there can be no doubt that history cumulates and abides. Indeed, why, or how, could we include history in the school curriculum if the past continuously ceases being the past? It is simply inconceivable, unimaginable that anybody could ever change or undo the past. Not even God could change the past. Whatever has happened in the past has happened whether or not we know it, and whether or not we properly interpret its meanings. Napoleon's defeat at Waterloo would remain a truth even if we all dropped dead, if no human beings were alive to talk about it or think of it as history. The fact that Napoleon existed is fixated in history forever; it is an absolute fact, totally unchangeable.

But of course, the pragmatist will allow no distinction between objective reality and human experience of reality. The minute he allowed this, he would become a realist; that is, he would be admitting that there are objective facts in reality that are not dependent upon our knowledge or affirmation of them. The pragmatist can easily *say* that there are no historical facts existing separately from our thoughts about them. I submit, however, that such a position is mere verbiage, for it is a reduction of all reality (both past and present) to nothing more than the thoughts now going on in our human minds (although, to be exact, the pragmatist will never definitely acknowledge the existence of a human mind). There is no pragmatist who can *practice* this principle, that reality is nothing more than what he produces in his own mind. I have yet to entice any pragmatist to admit that I exist outside of his mind. If he once definitely admitted this fact, that I am a separate being, a logically and existentially distinct agent, he would then be dumping his relativism and also his dogma of uncertainty. I have yet to hear any pragmatist admit that he exists, that he has a certain knowledge of this most obvious and given fact. It must surely seem incredible that anyone could sincerely doubt his own existence, for such doubt would seem both logically and psychologically impossible. In order to doubt at all, a person would first have to exist before he could do the doubting. Yet many of my colleagues persist in practicing this paper doubt and explain it with mumbo jumbo. It is no easy task persuading a pragmatist to concede that he exists in a world of other persons, creatures, and things.

Pragmatic sentiment is resolutely antiabsolutistic. In this school, the sin of sins is to hold that some truths are universal, that they are true independently of our consent or awareness. An absolute truth is a fact that is real, no matter who regards it as real or unreal, or who does or does not know it or care about it one way or another. For example, I hold, as a realist, that there is a past history subsisting independently of my knowledge, and that this is insusceptible to any reasonable doubt. Also, I hold that there are realities in the present world existing independently of my knowledge of them. These are facts that can be doubted only insincerely or in the pigheaded manner of an irrational sceptic. Indeed, this very certainty is the only guarantee against the insanity of solipsism. Were I to act seriously on the notion that only I exist, I would soon lose my bearings. Yet this very certainty, which is essential to every individual's sanity, is ruled out by the pragmatists as philosophical egocentrism and dogmatic closed-mindedness.

For example, Frederick Neff (who is about as professional a sceptic as can be found) insists:

The scientific spirit requires a man to be at all times ready to dump his whole cartload of beliefs, the moment experience is against them. The desire to learn forbids him to be perfectly cocksure that he knows already. Besides positive science can only rest on experience; and experience can *never* result in absolute certainty, exactitude, necessity, or universality. . . . to set up a philosophy which barricades the road of further advance toward the truth is the one unpardonable offence in reasoning. . . .[2]

Neff is quoting verbatim from Charles Peirce, in order to state his own view most effectively. Frankly, I find it impossible to imagine any person retaining his sanity if he ever "dumped" his "whole cartload of beliefs." That so radical and summary a rejection of one's past experience is possible is a very dubious assumption indeed. Surely there must be *some* facts, meanings, values, or perceptions in anyone's past life that were true and should be held onto in order to preserve the continuity and integrity of his identity. What is wrong with my being "cocksure" about the fact that I exist? What is wrong with refusing to doubt this, and many other things, which cannot really be doubted? What is wrong with simply giving the given credit for being the given? Can Neff explain how a psychiatrist could make a schizophrenic more socially realistic by acquiescing in his delusion that only he exists, or even that he might not exist at all?

Neff's (Peirce's) statement that "experience can *never* result in absolute certainty" is itself the expression of an absolute dogma, for it should be obvious that to employ the word "never" is to make a universal exclusion. This means that *no* person can ever have certain knowledge. The word "no" is universally exclusive. It binds you, me, and all before us and after us. In other words, all human beings without exception are permanently subject to the unvarying validity in this, Mr. Neff's judgment. Neff can have his own absolutes, but I, a nonpragmatist, must never have mine. He is absolutely certain that there can be no certainties.

This is a contradiction. Contradictions can never serve as a basis for philosophical validity, nor for intellectual humility. What is more, while claiming to renounce any and all absolute principles, the pragmatist establishes an absolute of his own out of change. He does this by insisting that change applies to *all* reality at *all* times. Unless it is definitely qualified, the word "all" is universally inclusive and cannot be a relativist term.

I cannot believe that intellectual humility should consist in this stubborn disposition to doubt all things. Nor should it consist in the unchanging dogma that all things constantly change. Intellectual humility must require the definite affirmation of *some* facts, principles, and values. Otherwise, humility would reduce down to mere scepticism and would undermine its own validity. An intellectually humble person need not pretend to doubt all things, nor to cultivate that kind of detachment in which he is supposedly protected from any abiding commitments. To be intellectually humble, one needs only to honor in all other persons the same prerogatives he honors in himself under the same circumstances. Has the pragmatist real humility in allowing himself a string of his own absolutes while berating the nonpragmatist for holding his absolutes aboveboard?

As for his dogma of change, the onus is on the pragmatist to prove the validity of this tenet, for it certainly is not a self-evident truth. For example, we might prevail upon him to prove that the laws of mathematics are constantly changing. If this could be done, no one would feel bound by numbers. There could be no valid mathematical principles or logic. We could compel no one to pass any mathematics exam. For in this case, mathematics would not be a science made up of facts. On the contrary, it would be only another branch of anthropology, i.e., just another mode in which the human imagination peculiarly and capriciously manifests itself. In a base ten counting system, two plus two could make four one moment, three the next, then five, etc.—but never necessarily add up to any figure at all.

How can the pragmatist prove that the *laws of logic* constantly change? John Dewey (*Lider Maximo* of the pragmatist forces) insists that the "laws of logic" have no objective validity outside the individual's thought. In a variety of books, he reduces logic to an "instrument" which the biological organism (a human being) invents to relieve its tensions, solve its problems, or escape "the insecurity accompanying an indeterminate situation." Every individual must invent his own logic to achieve "a satisfactory resolution or clarification" of his problems.[3] And since the individual's situations constantly change, it follows that his logic must also constantly change. According to Dewey, the laws of logic are a myth, if by this expression we mean anything other than the ideas that our biological drives force us to invent in order to adapt to our environment. I say this advisedly, however, since Dewey refuses to distinguish logically between the individual and his environment. From his point of view, all ideas are simply instruments for solving problems. Hence, he interprets "logical" ideas as those which enable him to adjust to his environment most "economically and efficiently."[4] He declares that "instrumentalism" (another term for pragmatism) means "a behaviorist theory of thinking and knowing. It means that knowing is literally something which we do."[5] The laws of logic do not exist outside of human knowing. And since "knowing is literally something which we do," there can be no logic except that which the organism invents to balance satisfactorily its own feelings and thoughts.

One would do Dewey an injustice if he accused him of insincerity. Apparently, few men ever tried harder to improve the teaching and learning conditions in American schools. He certainly must be given credit for striving toward objectivity. However, my trouble with him is: I can find no logic left after he reduces it to mere biology, and ends by equating the logical man with the biologically adjusted or socially satisfied man. Fearing it could lead to mere subjectivism, or capricious individualism, Dewey himself evidently sensed some fault in this theory. For he insists that objectivity is social agreement, especially among scientific observers. But unfortunately, the simple truth is that a whole society can be illogical and stupid in its reasoning, and so can a group of scientists. A contradiction does not become any less a contradiction just because a group of scientists or a prevailing majority of educated people happens to have it in its common reasoning. Dewey defines truth as "success in inquiry." He defines logic as those ideas with which the individual "reconstructs his experience." This means those ideas one uses to relate his present experiences with past ones in order to adjust successfully. Successful adjustment means a feeling of security, "satisfaction," "success in terminating an inquiry," or "solving a problem." Dewey then extends this feeling of satisfaction to society and equates objectivity with social satisfaction. He does this apparently to protect the social group from individual arbitrariness.

Even so, there are numerous objections to pragmatic logic, which many persons regard as exceedingly dangerous. For example, if logic consists only of those ideas that bring social satisfaction, then how can Dewey object to the hordes of people who are satisfied in their ignorance of their own contradictions? How can he object to the hordes of bigots, dema-gogues, and anti-intellectuals who have solid social backing? A realist affirms that the laws of logic subsist in reality in-dependently of our knowledge of them. Through reflective experience and education we can come to have a knowledge of these laws. We can discover them through intuition and reason. From the standpoint of reality, a person is irrational when he contradicts himself, regardless of whether or not he knows it or admits it. No amount of social sharing of irra-tionality can ever make it rational. In a variety of books, Dewey and his disciples vigorously plead for democracy. How-ever, they ignore the major questions and turn their backs on the serious criticisms of the assumption that social satis-faction or agreement is an adequate criterion of truth and goodness. From the standpoint of pragmatic logic, there can be no real distinction between moral truth and common mores. Neither can there be a distinction between right and might, as long as power rests in social consensus. There can be no distinction between truth and custom.

Pragmatists often criticize other people for being irrational and irresponsible. It is difficult to imagine how they have any right to do this, since by their own moorings they locate truth and logic nowhere except in biological adjustment and social satisfaction. To attribute irresponsibility and irrationality to anyone is to imply the existence of objective logic and moral values which the individual should know and live by whether he affirms them or not. This is to say, objective laws of logic and morality transcend mere personal opinion and taste. If this were not the case, then it would follow that any man would be rational who deemed himself rational. What is more, he would be right if he deemed himself right. Also, any society would be right if it had the power to impose its ideas on the dissenting individual.

I believe that if we affirmed this pragmatic logic, we simply would abandon philosophy and morality entirely. Or at least we would despair of any knowledge that is objectively rational and moral, for under such circumstances we would have lost all meaningful objective distinctions.

No sane philosophy of personal integrity can rest on such a basis. Sanity and integrity depend critically upon rational and moral inner order. But this is categorically impossible if the first assumption of pragmatism, that all things change, is true.

That all things change is an assumption no pragmatist ever lives by in practice, regardless of how mulishly he sticks to his dogma in theory. For first of all, there are the laws of nature whose constancy makes knowledge, predictability, and the sciences possible. Then, there are the various empirical facts of life which endure for certain lengths of time unchanged. For example, at the time I am writing this I am wearing a shirt and a tie—a fact that has not changed for hours. I am a resident of Colorado—a fact unchanged for months. There is a wedding ring on my left hand; its presence there has not changed for over four years. I am hundreds of dollars in debt—a fact that has not changed since . . . !

Listening to pragmatists talk, one would think that nature has no fixities, no structures, no fabric at all. If this were true, I could never find my way to my classes, for each new day their locality would change—the numbers on the doors would change, and the names of the streets would change. Whatever it is that makes *anything* identifiable would change—I could recognize no houses as such, streets as such, persons, trees, or dogs as such, for no structures at all could abide. Reality would have no beings or essences; therefore, no thing would be *essentially* different from anything else.

This is sheer nihilism. If pragmatism were true, my sanity could not abide. What is saddest of all, my love could not abide.

When the pragmatist is guileless, I can object only to his theory, his foundering in a dearth of common sense. But when he is militant and knows his own premises, then I must strenuously object to his spirit as brutal. He is saying that nothing is sacred. He is saying that nothing *can* and nothing *should* abide. This makes a mockery of love and is a denial of the importance of my God, my self, and my friends.

2.

The Mind: "Only
a Name"

PRAGMATISM'S second principle, that *all values and truths are relative, individual, and temporary,* is also suicidal. In this dogma another unconscious absolute inheres in the use of the word "all." If "all" values and truths are relative, then no single exception is allowed, and we have made just as binding a universal dogma as if we were frankly realistic and acknowledged our own absolutes. The word "all" is universally inclusive. Any judgment employing this term is an absolutist judgment, no matter how skillfully the pragmatist may evade recognition of his logical contradiction. In simple fairness, it would seem that the pragmatist should not ride in the same bus with the absolutists since he roundly condemns them all en route.

A realist does not hesitate to acknowledge that there are relative truths. There certainly are many realities that men and other creatures invent, both as individuals and *en suite.* That is to say, there are many realities which are directly dependent for their existence upon the arbitrary judgments and actions of individual creatures and groups. We create many realities which exist not necessarily but because we freely invent them, and their existence is dependent upon our will. For example, I designed and constructed a house whose existence is contingent upon my will that it exist. If I decided to destroy the house, it would then go out of being; its existence is plainly relative to my own existence, not to mention the existence of other persons.

There are innumerable other facts in the world whose existence is dependent upon passing persons and things, upon time or change. The realist does not ignore the reality of this change in the world. He simply rejects the pragmatic dogma that *all* things are changing, or that nothing abides. He sees that we live in a world in which some things change and some do not. There are both temporary realities and permanent realities. There are both *sui generis* realities and realities that are strictly relative to powers beyond themselves. Some things exist necessarily (as ends in themselves), and some things exist unnecessarily, or in the strictest contingency. For example, the laws of logic subsist independently of all things. Their reality is not in any way dependent upon the will of any creatures or forces that be.

The same thing can be said for the laws of mathematics, which subsist everlastingly and transcend the creative and destructive powers of all men. Of course, we should acknowledge that men in different societies invent different symbols, or language, with which to record and communicate these laws to one another. In English, one says, "In a base ten system two plus two equals four." In Spanish, one says, "Dos y dos son cuatro." Thus, the existence of mathematical language obviously is relative to different peoples in different cultures, and to different times. Any individual's knowledge of mathematical realities (or, for that matter, of any other realities) certainly is relative to (1) his capacity to learn, (2) his opportunity to learn, and (3) his willingness or unwillingness to learn. Indeed, it may be said definitely that *all* our knowledge of reality is relative to our experience, and our experience is relative to these aforementioned things. However, it is one thing to make our knowledge contingent upon our experience of reality, as the realist does; it is quite another to make all reality dependent upon human knowledge, as the relativist does. The pragmatist regards the laws of mathematics as *inventions* of human minds. He will grant no objective validity or reality to these laws outside of relative human thoughts. This is to say in effect that if all mathematicians suddenly went to sleep or died, there would be no mathematical laws at all in reality.

The realist regards this view as extremely egocentric. Indeed, this is a grossly anthropomorphic kind of philosophizing, for it reduces all reality to dependence on human subjectivity which, pragmatism teaches, is governed by no objective laws of any kind. From the standpoint of realism, even the operations of the mind must be subject to some laws. All of us have some freedom, some capacity to operate spontaneously, in making choices that are creative, not lawful or predetermined. Truly, a philosophy of responsible moral autonomy would be impossible if this capacity for free choice were not real.

But equally so, all of us are subject to certain psychological laws in the way we must think and act as human beings. For example, all of us perceive the world of things and events in terms of cause and effect. We see that certain events happen *after* other events happen, which in turn happen *before* others happen, etc. We think in terms of relations and sequence, i.e., in terms of space and time. Also, all of us think in terms of consistency and coherency, at least to some extent. If I said, "I went to town last night," but a moment later said, "I stayed at home last night and did not go out," even an imbecile would immediately know that I was contradicting myself. As human beings, we need and strive for coherency. Even when we deceive and contradict ourselves, we strive for some form of coherency or personal unity, in our efforts to hide our contradictions. Even in insanity there is some struggle for unity. The restricted coherency of insanity is the result of one's attempt to escape from a world he fears would destroy his unity altogether. Fearing that the world would explode his being, one retreats from it to save the unity he knows no other way to preserve. In health, one has a dialogue with himself and the world; but in insanity, one's dialogue is in isolation, with himself alone.

That all human beings have an essential need for coherency, pragmatism must in theory deny. For in denying that there are essences in the world, the pragmatist is in effect also denying that there are any meaningful realities. There certainly can be no "nature" or "human nature" if there are no essences whereby human beings are essentially different from other creatures and things. If there are no essences in reality, as the pragmatist assumes, then surely there can be no humanness, no needs and attributes that all of us have in common. Relativism strips nature of all its distinctions, simply because it denies in theory that a human being is different from a dog, a house, or a tree. According to realism, if I am to be regarded as different from a tree, then both I and the tree must be constituted of different essences. Although we may possess some essences in common, the tree and I must have some essences that are different. Otherwise, neither of us can be an individual with a distinct nature of his own. If relativism were really true, how could anyone distinguish me from a tree or a house? How can we talk meaningfully of individual identity, or personal autonomy, if none of us has any essences whereby he is distinguishable from other persons and things? What calling is there for integrity if we have no *essential* need for coherency and unity in our experiences of life?

There are many persons who call themselves relativists but are not acquainted with the formal premises of this doctrine. Many do not understand what they are saying with their doltish cliché, "All things are relative." On the other hand, there are the professional philosophers who have produced and cultivated the tenets of relativism, and I think it would follow that if their tenets were true, any discussion of the principles of moral autonomy would be concretely meaningless. Already, I have accused relativism of dissolving the individual because it has denied that any one of us exists in essence distinct from other persons and things in the world. I think it will become apparent that relativism does this, as I present its tenets in the way the relativists themselves have stated them.

These tenets are:

1. All reality is a system of relations.
2. Every quality is a system of relations.
3. Every object, thing, or person is a system of relations.
4. All relations are "internal"; i.e., relations do not just occur between objects, for objects do not exist apart from or independently of their relations. All objects and qualities are themselves constituted of their relations.

5. No object or quality exists in and of itself, in any way independently of other objects and qualities.
6. Parts have no real existence independently of the whole, and all parts are determined by the whole.
7. In reality, there are no merely "external" relations between objects. There are no independent terms or variables, for all relations (i.e., qualities or things) are mutually dependent and reciprocally determined.
8. Nothing exists that is not influenced and determined by other things.
9. Likewise, nothing exists that does not influence and partially determine everything else.
10. Everything overlaps and interfuses with everything else. The whole permeates all the parts, just as every part diffuses into the whole.
11. Nothing exists *sui generis,* i.e., with a definitely individual or separate nature, being, or essence.
12. When anything at all is changed, everything in the universe is changed, for the simple reason that everything is relative to everything else.
13. Because everything is constantly changing, there can be no fixed realities, hence no certain knowledge.
14. Truly to know or understand anything, one would have to understand everything perfectly, for nothing can exist with a separate and independent nature of its own, or be definitely knowable in and of itself, or by itself.
15. There can be no logical or existential distinction between cause and effect. Neither cause nor effect is prior to or different from the other. Therefore, all relations are internal, and reality is a pure continuum or one whole.

The above tenets represent the general doctrine of relativism, that is, the doctrine that all relations in the universe are "internal." One finds this doctrine expressed explicitly or implicitly in the writings of all the pragmatists. For example, with regard to change, Frederick Neff declares, "If there is any measure of 'reality' or 'energy of being' it is no longer fixity but omnipresent change."[1]

Regarding the interfusion of continually changing things, pragmatist Donald Arnstine defines the human mind as an "environmental interaction" and then reduces the environment and the individual to one and the same thing. Refusing to distinguish his mind from his environment, Mr. Arnstine offers us a typically pragmatic definition of mind, namely, "a term indicating a particular way that a person and his environment are related." He further states that

it would make no sense to say that certain properties "belong" to the environment, and certain others to mind. It would make no sense because any properties that belonged to the one would, in the nature of things, belong equally to the other at the same time. . . . Properties belong neither to one nor the other, but to both. Yet the term "both" does not refer, here, to two things. Rather, it refers to but one thing: an interacting field in which theoretical distinctions ("mind" and "environment") are made in order to facilitate communication and action. . . .

The ascription of a property is a direct function of perception. The property belongs not to an object, but is a function of a field. The perception would appear to be in us. But the world is not made up of perceptions *and* properties which can be assigned each to their proper location. Perceptions are always *of* properties (or of relations, such as our seeing that George is taller than Harold). Hence the perception which appeared to be in us is not in us at all but—since it is itself indissolubly bound to the entire field—is itself an event within a field of events. . . .

Because any event allegedly internal to an individual—that is, a property or function of his mind—is, in fact, a function of an entire field with which an individual interacts, it is proper to say that all mental events, or properties, or functions of mind—are simply natural events. . . .[2]

Here, the fact is indeed obvious that relativism interfuses all realities into one. Arnstine states that the color "brown is not a property somewhere out in an environment, nor is a reminiscence an event inside of a mind. Brownness and the reminiscence are both simply events that have occurred as a result of the interaction of a field. . . . The events in question are perceptions, feelings, and thoughts. All the perceptions, feelings, and thoughts a person has are relative to him."³

Inevitably, the pragmatist must revert to realism in spite of himself. In the preceding quotes, is it not obvious that Mr. Arnstine implies the existence of particular individuals who are logically and existentially separate from one another? For example, he says:

> Since a perception is always *of* a property, and a feeling is always *about* something, they incorporate aspects of both environment and this or that particular person. Because of this, there is no avoiding the conclusion that *every perception is relative to him who has it.* Each one of my perceptions—which is to say, the pervasive quality of every moment of my entire life—is unique to *me* and is, therefore, probably different in quality from each one of *your* perceptions.⁴

It is unfortunate that a philosopher must deny common-sense distinctions between the individual and his environment, while at the same time frequently and unavoidably referring to them as though they were valid distinctions. Such seesawing between relativism and realism can never possibly lead to a coherent philosophy of reality. On the contrary, it can breed only ambiguity and confusion. For example, Mr. Arnstine first analyzes away the individual, saying that he has no concrete reality except in other persons and things. The result of this is a vicious circle; for, in the same relativism, the other persons and things also have no concrete reality except in him. Clearly referring to "this or that particular person" (as though particular persons really *exist*), Arnstine then proceeds to make the existence of a real individual a theoretical and existential impossibility. For we must remember that he states categorically:

> what we call mind and environment are not separate entities, but rather are only the *names* we give to practical distinctions we make within a total field. Perceptions, feelings, and thoughts are *called* mental events only for similar, practical reasons, but in fact "belong" no more to mind than they do to the environment. They are simply events, and mind, far from being a ghostly container of these events, is simply the term we use to refer to particular kinds of ways in which people interact with their environment.⁵

From the above quotes, it becomes apparent that Mr. Arnstine is generally a realist in practice but a relativist in his theory. For the truth is that no person can go through life denying the logical and existential distinction between himself as an individual and other persons and things, *in practice*. It is only in nebulous theory that the relativist can interfuse all persons and things and abstractly make them one. In his theory (which holds no logical cogency), the relativist reduces the whole to the parts; but then, he dissolves the parts into the whole and ends by effacing any meaningful distinction between the separate parts, or between any particular part and the whole.

As quoted earlier, Arnstine says, "It would make no sense to say that certain properties 'belong' to the environment, and certain others to mind." He further insists that "perceptions, feelings, and thoughts . . . in fact 'belong' no more to mind than they do to the environment." This simply means that we must not look upon an individual's mind and his environment as truly distinguishable realities. Here speaking like a realist, Arnstine refers to the "particular person," as though the particular person is real, with perceptions which are his own, and which, therefore, are individual, separate, and not to be confused existentially or logically with the perceptions of distinctly other individuals. But then, he puts on his hat and afterward cuts off his head, saying, "The perception which appeared to be in us is not in us at all . . .—since it is itself indissolubly bound to the entire field," and every "event allegedly internal to an individual . . . is, in fact, a function of an entire field. . . ."

If he intends for us to take him seriously, what possible meaning can he have in mind when he tells us that "every perception is relative to *him* who *has* it"?[6] On the one hand, he tells us that "each one of *my* perceptions . . . is unique to *me* and is, therefore, probably different in quality from each one of *your* perceptions."[7] This sounds realistic, and it is perfectly plausible; it acknowledges the existence of separate individuals, each one of whom has experiences that belong uniquely to him. In reality, Mr. Arnstine and I are separately existing, distinct agents; he has his perceptions and I have mine. But then, he insists on the other hand that "the world is not made up of perceptions *and* properties which can be assigned each to their proper location." In other words, he is telling us that there are in reality no individual subjects and objects characterized by qualities which simply are what they are. There are no things in the universe that are actually distinguishable one from the other.

We might ask him, If perceptions and qualities cannot be "assigned" to individual subjects and objects, or to individual experiences, then where are they to be found at all? How can I have my perceptions, and Arnstine his, if perceptions cannot be located in distinctly individual agents? In behalf of consistency, how can he say that perceptions belong to nobody and at the same time say that "every perception is relative to him who *has* it"?[8] If I may repeat, he says, "Each one of my perceptions . . . is . . . different in quality from each one of your perceptions." But, conversely, he insists that no perception or property can belong to anyone or enjoy a "proper location." In fact, he insists that "the perception which appeared to be in us is not in us at all."

Here, I must protest against his flagrant violations of common sense and logic. If no perception can be located in the individual perceiver (which Arnstine insists is the case), then how can perception in any way be "relative" to the person who "has" it? How can there be individual perceptions if perception "is itself indissolubly bound to the entire field"? If Arnstine's argument were true, only the whole (the "entire field") could see, hear, think, and will. Different persons simply could not exist to have different perceptions, or to will and think as individuals.

The chief fallacy of relativism lies in its semantical perversion, its assigning of reality to terms only to deny that the selfsame terms are real. First, it postulates the existence of an "environment," then the existence of an individual's "mind." Thereupon, it defines both of them as an "interaction" with each other, while denying that either has any concrete reality of its own. Arnstine says: "Properties belong neither to one nor the other, but to both. Yet the term 'both' does not refer, here, to two things. Rather, it refers to but one thing: an interacting field in which theoretical distinctions ('mind' and 'environment') are made in order to facilitate communication and action."

My questions are: Who makes these distinctions if no individuals really exist who can make them? Since when have I, a living individual, become only an artificial distinction made by an "entire field" just to "facilitate" some impersonal "communication and action"? If individual agents are a myth, then to whom can we assign responsibility for human thoughts and choices?

Without further quotations, it should appear obvious that relativism eradicates any genuine distinction between the individual and his environment. For the sake of an empty theory, filled with contradictions, relativism dissolves the individual into his social relations. It leaves each of us as nothing but a barren abstraction in an "interacting field." According to Arnstine, the individual is in reality only a term of "convenience" which "refers to no real distinction between supposedly independent entities."[9] In fine, our existence as individual agents is a mere abstraction, a semantical illusion.

This is a theory that no person can ever live by in practice. What is more, it castrates logic by totally undermining the law of identity. If the parts have no real properties *as parts,* distinguishable from other parts and the whole, then no definite distinctions are allowable at all. Certainly, no subjects or objects can possess definite meaning if no definite properties or qualities belong to them and set them off for what they are. Nor can they have any meaning if they do not exist as realities in themselves. If the terms of relations are unreal, surely the relations themselves must be unreal. Or, if the terms of relations are unreal, yet the relations themselves are real, we end with nothing except relations between relations, which is sheer ambiguity.

Since when is a simple quality a "system of relations"? Why can we not regard qualities simply as qualities? For example, why isn't redness simply redness? If all qualities "mutually and reciprocally determine each other," how can we distinguish redness from greenness? If redness and greenness mutually and reciprocally determine each other, then am I to believe that redness determines greenness, but also greenness determines redness? Since this is categorically nonsensical, am I to conclude that there are no such distinguishable colors in the world? The pragmatist believes there can be no separate qualities or essences in reality, with each quality simply *being what it is,* in and of itself. Consequently, it follows that there can be no redness that is *in essence* different from greenness.

To a realist, such thinking as this would seem completely to mortify philosophy. The purpose of philosophy should be to discover and sustain meaningful distinctions, rather than to abolish them. If all realities mutually and reciprocally determined each other, would not goodness determine evil, and evil determine goodness? Would not rationality determine irrationality and unreason reason? Would not vulgarity determine beauty, and beauty determine vulgarity? As a realist, I certainly should insist that these contrasting values are related to each other, for they are real and exist in the same world. However, it is one thing to say that different realities are *related* in the world; it is altogether another to interfuse them and destroy their logically distinct meanings by making them "mutually and reciprocally determined." If goodness and evil mutually constituted each other, we would lose all meaningful moral distinctions.

We gain nothing in understanding by denying that there are distinct essences and beings in the world. In reading Hook's *Quest for Being,* we note how the pragmatist attempts to deny real meaning to these terms. However, it is impossible to find any pragmatist who does not continuously employ these terms in all his writings. Here, Hook unconsciously affirms the validity of what he consciously denies, that is, the presence of real essences in the world. None less than pragmatism's paterfamilias, John Dewey, presents a whole book on *Individualism and the Individual,* in which he honors the existence of real, individual agents *in practice,* and in real life establishes the falsity of his relativist dogmas. In theory, however, he holds strictly to the doctrine of internal relations. Dewey's world is ontologically a whole. He treats all reality as a "pure continuum" and allows no distinction between subject and object, knower and known, and cause and effect.[10]

There is no evidence whatever that a change in anything results necessarily in a change in everything. If the dogma of internal relations were true, then of course this would be the case. However, there is abundant evidence that many relations in the world are merely external, which means that while the external relations between things change, the things in themselves, between which the relations inhere or occur, may not change at all. For example, an owner of two automobiles may drive one of them without touching or getting near the other. The fact that the driven car moves away from the other creates a change in the distance (external relation) between the two cars. But in this case, the parked car is in no way affected (internally changed, or changed in its own nature) by the fact that the other car is being driven.

Also, there are external relations between human beings and other living creatures. Someone may die or be born in another country, and it is possible that in an entire lifetime we may never do anything that makes us known to each other, or that even indirectly effects a change in either one of us. Indeed, even in an intimate life between two lovers, some relations are internal and some are merely external. For example, my wife and I continuously effect changes in each other's states of feeling or thought. Our ideas and actions effect changes in each other's moods, etc. However, the fact that we have intimate spiritual and sexual relations has not changed the fact that I am a man and my wife is a woman. I have not become feminine through these relations, nor has Nancy become masculine. My essential nature in this respect has remained unchanged, and so has hers. The fact that we interrelate has not changed the fact that each of us is a separate agent.

It is curious that relativism prides itself so greatly on its "respect to the individual." It often rules out realism and idealism as tyrannical and autocratic philosophies, as, for example, when Frederick Neff writes: "Pragmatic education is unequivocally a philosophy of democratic education, whereas other educational theories might apply with equal effectiveness to aristocratic and totalitarian ways of life."[11]

It is difficult for me to grasp how any particular political philosophy can be logically derived from pragmatism. This would seem especially true if we defined a democracy as a way of life which affirms that some values are *essentially* better than others—for example, open-mindedness is better than closed-mindedness, freedom of thought better than tyranny, and freedom for creativity better than stifling conformity. I should think pragmatism could not possibly serve as a logical basis for democracy if we consider the fact that it categorically and persistently denies that reality has any essences or intrinsic values. Pragmatism denies that any way of life is *in essence* better than any other. Hence, it refutes its own premise that a democratic way of life is better than tyranny. After it abolishes all meaningful distinctions, pragmatism cannot stand for any *definite* principles, values, or truths whatever. Indeed, I include a discussion of it in this book for the precise reason that it is a doctrine logically inimical to any essential order, essential moral laws, and fails to recognize the essential reality of separate individuals. Under the terms of relativism, all individuals vanish into unreality. Everybody is liquefied into a dull oneness, into a meaningless "entire field," an equivocal whole. We can neither theoretically nor practically do justice to a human being by analyzing him away. If I am a mere abstraction, a mere "term of convenience" produced by the whole, then I can have no autonomy whatever.

The most essential idea to a philosophy of autonomy is the individual's freedom of will to choose. But how can anyone make free choices if he does not concretely exist as a free agent? How can one *be* an individual if one is but a bare abstraction produced by the gross action of an "entire field"? How can there be an individual agent responsible for his own free choices if all of us are only products of an all-governing whole?

Clearly, relativism undermines all moral responsibility simply by removing it from real individuals, then assigning it to something entirely beyond all of us—to some impersonal, gross force.

Dewey, for example, insists that individual minds are a myth. We traditionalists are naïve, he says, in assuming that thought is personal, that it belongs to individuals or is produced by individual minds. He tells us:

In first instance and intent, it is not exact nor relevant to say "I experience" or "I think." "It" experiences or is experienced, "it" thinks or is thought, is a juster phrase. Experience, a serial course of affairs with their own characteristic properties and relationships, occurs, happens, and is what it is. Among and within these occurrences, not outside of them nor underlying them, are those events which are denominated selves.[12]

He further states:

. . . one can hardly use the term "experience" in philosophical disclosure, but a critic rises to inquire *"Whose* experience?" The question is asked in adverse criticism. Its implication is that experience by its very nature is owned by some one; and that the ownership is such in kind that everything about experience is affected by a private and exclusive quality.[13]

Thus, Dewey unmistakably reduces the personal agent to a flow of impersonal experience and denies that experience is private and belongs to particular individuals. According to him, experience is antecedent to the existence of subjects and objects and to any qualities in the world. Dewey's disciple, pragmatist Lawrence Thomas, attempts to explain this point of view by stating that

experience does not *discover* or disclose objects antecedently given. Rather his experience *achieves* objects, by differentiation and abstraction. . . .experience is a basic, primary condition, logically prior to either subjects or objects. Experience, in Dewey's words, "recognizes in its primary integrity no division between act and material, subject and object, but contains them both in an unanalyzed totality." Instead of starting with a subject who *has* experiences, experimentalism (pragmatism) starts with an experiencing process which can, upon analysis, be differentiated into subjects and objects. . . .Subjects and objects are twin-born in the differentiating transactions of on-going experience.[14]

Now here, one may well raise a question of priority, namely, How is it logically possible to derive the personal from the impersonal, or the meaningful from the meaningless?

But Thomas continues:

Pragmatism takes the undifferentiated flow of experience as the starting point for philosophic thought. . . .The nature of the object consists of the relationships which both connect it to and distinguish it from the perceiving subject and other perceived objects in the environment. Similarly, any inquiry into the nature of the subject's self requires explicit reference to surrounding conditions. His selfhood consists of relationships with environments of the past, present, and anticipated future. In short, when the ultimate nature of one's self and one's environment is sought, the experimentalist finds that they *dissolve* into relationships within the flow of experience.[15]

Here again, we find the individual agent ultimately stripped of any capacity for autonomous existence and action. As Thomas clearly admits, the individual is "dissolved" into an ongoing flow of impersonal "experience." This experience, he says, is universal; it is prior to the existence of any subjects or objects and belongs to no agent, either finite or infinite. It somehow "achieves" all subjects and objects and somehow "differentiates" between them, while all subjects and objects are nevertheless in reality *one.*

Thomas betrays a consciousness of the difficulty our common sense has in accepting this view. In fact, he realizes that it makes no logical sense to a realist, and he even admits that it is unscientific. For experience, he says, is prior to all empirical and logical distinctions. When asked what this experience is, that is devoid of properties or essences by which it can be known, he admits that it is beyond the knowable and calls it "The Given." But the question is, What right has he to call it "The Given" since by his own insistence it has no definite, meaningful, knowable, or given properties? To this question, we receive the slighting and evasive answer: *"This is the kind of problem Dewey once recommended solving by turning one's back on it.*[16]

It is interesting to note that Dewey rejects the idea of God because it is, he says, subject to no empirical verification and is, therefore, intellectually meaningless. God can in no way be measured or proved by experimental means, for he is totally intangible, hence is a meaningless hypothesis. For the same reasons, Dewey rejects the idea of an individual mind or soul. He insists that the soul is a scientifically useless concept because it has no empirically assessable properties; it cannot be located and is beyond observation. In fact, Dewey professes to reject all the concepts and postulates of any philosophy that cannot be tested and verified by strictly scientific procedures. Since this is the case, is he not acting on an unfair prerogative, viz., accepting as valid his own concept of "undifferentiated experience," which can in no way be empirically observed? Dewey objects to my taking my *soul* as The Given. On the grounds that no one can observe his spirit in a scientific manner, he objects to my regarding myself as an agent. Indeed, my spirit has no tangible dimensions, no height, depth, width, hardness, color, or weight. Nothing about it can be empirically observed or measured. No one can touch, taste, smell, see, or hear a spirit. For these reasons, Dewey rejects both God and the soul. Yet in the same breath he requires that we accept his "pure experience," which belongs to no one, transcends all conceptualization and feeling, and evades all analysis.

This is the hypocrisy of pragmatism: the doctrine accepts its own unverified assumptions as the truth while pretending to be purely scientific. And all the while, it allows none of its adversaries the right to do the same.

In summary, I must object to relativism on both logical and personal grounds. Logically, the doctrine reduces all conceptual thinking to a vicious circle, for it destroys any meaningful distinction between relations and the terms of relations. It undermines any distinction between objects and their relations. For example, I go to buy a car and find that I must choose between a blue Cougar and a red Charger. But how can I make a choice if the two cars are not separate entities, essentially different from each other, and made up of separately existing and unique parts? How can I choose between a red car and a blue one if they and all other things interfuse to make one? How can I distinguish redness from blueness, or choose between colors, if there are no color qualities existing separately and independently of each other, between which I can choose? Or, how can I choose a satisfactory partner to work with if persons do not exist as real agents, with distinguishable moral and immoral characteristics in their individual natures?

We do violence to reality when we try to reduce real qualities to relations. No quality can be reduced to relations without thereupon evaporating and losing its meaning as a definite and distinct term of reality.

I object to relativism's unfeeling suffocation of the individual's spirit. A human being is no mere abstraction, and no mere series of acts in some impersonal "process of becoming." Of course, each of us is or should be striving to enrich his identity and experience of life. But this ever-present fact of striving is no evidence that we are not already human. It reduces man to something less than what he really is to say that he is only "becoming." If I am only becoming human, but not yet *am,* then how shall I be reclassified? If I am not human, then what *am* I?

This unfortunate doctrine would de-individualize and depersonalize the human being by decomposing his concrete existence. To be a real individual or person, one must be logically and *existentially* a unique agent who is separate and distinct in his being and acting. To be consistent, the relativist must tell me that I am not real, and that I have no importance or worth as an individual in and of myself. From the premises of relativism, it follows that there can be no reality, and no value, except in that obscure and indefinite soup called "the social milieu" or the "entire field." I, as a human being per se, am nothing and am worth nothing.

Yet, the pragmatists tell us that it is *they* who believe in democracy!

Certainly, one must honor their right to theorize as they wish, as long as they do not roll over us as nonentities *in practice*.

It is indeed difficult to understand how relativism can be a basis for true democracy.

3.

The One Certainty:
Uncertainty

IF I CORRECTLY assess the national situation, the majority of American professors of philosophy of education are pragmatists. I may be mistaken in this assumption, for I must admit that my judgment is not founded in any poll or close survey of the nation's universities and colleges. It is just that, wherever I go, I find most of my colleagues who are teaching in that department to be self-avowed relativists. My present department is the only exception I have found. In every conference I have attended, the majority of speakers have taken the pragmatic stance.

As I mentioned earlier, I do not see how a viable philosophy of autonomy is possible if the fundamental tenets of this doctrine are true. Therefore, in this chapter I shall continue to criticize them and point out how they would whip down the individual and affront his dignity if he allowed himself to take them seriously.

Like the others, the third principle of pragmatism seems to refute itself.[1] This principle states that *all human judgments are arbitrary, fallible, and uncertain.*

Actually, pragmatists seldom, if ever, use the term "principle." They prefer to use the term "assumption," since this sounds more in keeping with their dogmatic belief that no one can have certain or definite knowledge of any truth. Perhaps we should close our eyes here in order that the pragmatist in his antiabsolutism may save face. He surely must be embarrassed if he dares to see that, once again, he has offered us only another absolute of his own. That "all" human judgments are fallible would include mine, yours, and everybody else's all the time; hence, it plainly would allow no exceptions whatever to this pragmatic dogma. This is an obvious contradiction. For precisely what is wrong with belief in absolutes, says the pragmatist, is the fact that reality is totally relative; and therefore, we must allow no principles that are without exception. Although he is of course unconscious of this fact, the relativist must employ an absolute every time he denies an absolute. This is to say: if there are no absolutes in reality, then there absolutely are no absolutes, for the word "no" is universally exclusive. This is scarcely safe ground to stand on for one who would be an honest intellectual. Since when may the pragmatist employ as many absolutes as he wishes in order to safeguard his certain position that there can be no certain position?

Does it not ill become a professional philosopher to say that *all* human judgments are arbitrary? Obviously, if all our judgments are arbitrary, this pragmatic tenet itself must be merely arbitrary; that is, it can have no ground whatever in factuality or logic; consequently, we should not take it seriously because it denies its own validity. A realist never denies that some, or many, of our judgments are arbitrary, fallible, and uncertain. Any person who has really lived must have learned that human beings can experience illusions, make premature judgments, and reach erroneous conclusions on the counsel of inadequate evidence and untested assumptions. What is more, we often think and act in willfully prejudicial ways. This obvious truth needs no argument or proof. But we would be stretching a rubber band into a cosmic inner tube if we concluded from this that human beings can *never* have any definite or certain knowledge of reality.

We know, beyond any feasible doubt, that the earth is a finite body. We know that it is basically spheroid in shape, and that it bulges at the equator due to the centrifugal force from the earth's spinning on its axis, which causes the area around the equator to swell. We have photographs of the earth, taken from outer space, which prove that this is the truth. I have traveled several times around the earth and learned from experience that it is not a cube with a flat surface, as some primitive peoples even to this day believe. We know that there was a time when probably all human beings regarded the earth as "flat." There was a unanimous judgment that the earth was in a state of rest, that night and day were caused by the sun's revolving around a motionless earth. However, there can be no reasonable doubt now that these primitive beliefs were erroneous (however sincere), and that, due to inadequate experience in studying the earth and its neighbors (the telescope had not yet been invented, nor had Copernicus been born), such beliefs were false simply because they did not correspond with the objective truth that the earth is round and in motion. The truth was: the earth was round and people *thought* that it was a flat-surfaced cube. But their thinking that it was a cube did not *make* it a cube. Objective truth consists of those realities in the universe with which we have to cope.

Objective truth limits, binds, and determines what we can be, do, and know, whether or not we realize it and whether or not we care about it. A realistic philosopher must insist that there is a distinction between a subjective belief and an objective truth. In some primitive tribes in the world today people still have the subjective belief that the earth is flat. But to the enlightened man, there can be no doubt that in objective reality their belief is false. An intelligible concept of progress in education presupposes that, through experience, we can continuously overcome false, subjective beliefs with true, objective knowledge, as we acquire tools and skills with which to assess reality more accurately. If we take primitive men from their tribes and introduce them successfully to the learning of more advanced culture, they invariably come to realize that their judgment of the earth's shape was in error.

As I earlier noted, no realist would deny that all human knowledge is relative to the individual's experience. The primitive man's belief about the shape of the earth is different from ours simply because his experience is different from ours and more limited. The fact that the earth is a finite body, with a finite mass, is not susceptible to a reasonable doubt; for if the earth were an infinite body, with an infinite mass, then clearly it would be the only body in existence and would occupy all space. An infinite body could have no discontinuance, no limitations, hence no surface upon which we could walk. There could be no other planets or stars, in fact, no space or sky.

But of course, the persistent pragmatist would immediately reply: "Oh, but what if the earth does not exist, except in people's minds? I mean, what if it is only a figment of one's imagination? And since each person's imagination is different, then there must be as many different shapes to the earth as there are imaginations!"

This little game is perhaps not as clever as the pragmatist would like us to believe. There is something essentially obtuse in fictitious retreats from reality that are grounded in practical contradictions. First of all, there is the fact that no person can take seriously the notion of the physical unreality of the hard earth, *in practice*. The earth is a physical effect. It is not merely a thought or a feeling. No one's head would be smashed if he jumped out a window onto the hard sidewalk only in a dream. But if in an actual state one jumps and lands on a concrete sidewalk twenty stories below, then he does *not* land on a mere sensation or on a figment of his imagination. In reality, the earth is *there,* outside of one's mind, and it can break one's bones, even end one's life.

Second, there is the logical contradiction inherent in relativism's purely subjective theory. According to this view, the earth exists only in subjectivity, i.e., with different shapes in different persons' perceptions or imaginations. As an object in and of itself, the earth does not exist. In a certain primitive man's mind the earth is a cube. In my own mind it is basically a sphere. In another primitive person's mind, the earth is a flat surface which extends on and on, in every direction, without any end in space. Nevertheless, it is logically incompatible that the earth, as an object, can be at the same time a finite and an infinite body, a spheroid and a cube. Either there is an objective earth, which is a planet existing as an object independently of our thought, and its shape *is* what it *is;* or else, there is in reality nothing more than subjectivity, and it is riddled with the irrationality of incompatible imaginations and perceptions. If we accept relativism, we must do so at the expense of an objective logic; we must end without any objective knowledge about the earth at all. Earth scientists become only myth-makers, just as astronomers become a chorus of arbitrary poets.

The assumption that a human being is *always* fallible is utter nonsense. How can any human go through life and never, at any time, definitely *know* anything? The implication here is that we are always at least one remove from reality, one step away from any true knowledge about anything in the universe. If knowledge were really this difficult to acquire, then indeed, we should acknowledge that we can know nothing at all. It should be obvious, however, that this is a contradiction, for either we know that we do not know anything, or else we do not and cannot know it. But to say that we know we do not know anything obviously is to affirm what we claim to deny. The logical implication of this pragmatic dogma is that all of us should become universal sceptics. Since we cannot be certain of anything, we must be uncertain of everything.

This is a dose of pragmatism too biting for the realist's stomach. There is no evidence that a person can *always* be wrong. Such an assumption is radically unempirical, and no rational person can believe it for a moment. If we were to take this dogma seriously, we would bog down in the grossest contradiction of which the human mind is capable.

To be sure, no human being can become functionally autonomous without much critical reflection and doubt. Every man needs to relate with himself honestly, and this requires a mature habit of self-questioning and self-evaluation. Open-mindedness is essential to autonomy, for without it one would face the constant danger of self-complacency and that kind of ignorance which makes an expanding personal identity impossible. An identity that is afraid to expand, or is too lazy to expand, can represent at best only a very weak and limited kind of autonomy. Even insane persons have varying degrees of real autonomy. No person, either sane or insane, is capable of doubting or rejecting *everything* about himself and his world. Even the most serious act of suicide entails some affirmation. One would not act to end his life without in some sense affirming the desirability of the act. No person can become totally disunified or out of contact with himself. There is no agent who ever ceases being an agent, as long as he is alive. I know of no man who is totally devoid of accountability for his motives and acts. The behaviorists and phenomenologists disavow the reality of man as an agent, for they inevitably reduce the human spirit to a biological or social product; or, like Sartre, they reduce the source of his being to nothing and make his existence purely happenstance and meaningless.

Today, there are whole schools of psychologists who regard the free agent as a "semantical illusion," a myth. If I am not mistaken, they are probably in the majority of psychiatrists and psychologists who either teach or practice professionally. But fortunately, there are also many who affirm the reality of the spirit and its inherent capacity to make free choices. In fact, some go even so far as to say that a human being can *freely* decide to efface his own capacity for making free choices, that is, through a progressive series of free decisions one can gradually suffocate his own will or capacity to act freely. For example, one can make so many cowardly decisions that he eventually evolves into the *complete* coward. One may willfully enshrine himself with the self-image and self-concept of The Coward, from which he has decidedly convinced himself he can never escape or change. Thus, instead of being conditioned by external forces to be a coward, he has freely conditioned himself, and ends up as the victim of his own conditioning.

That self-conditioning of either a constructive or destructive kind can be done by the free individual is a truth essential to the whole concept of personal autonomy; for surely, no one can be autonomous except to the extent that he is capable of directing himself and determining his own destiny. Without freedom to choose between responsible and irresponsible ways of acting, one would act only instinctively or mechanically; hence, he could no more be responsible for himself than could a combustion engine. He could attribute to himself neither merit nor guilt, neither dignity nor indignity, unless he could choose between these things. For if he could not possibly act in undignified ways, neither could he have a dignity for which he himself was responsible by choice.

However, I doubt that those psychologists are right who say that a person can completely blot out his freedom. Rather, if one is born with an inherent capacity to choose between the alternatives confronting him, it would seem that, however much he might abuse his own potentialities, he nevertheless would retain *some* of this capacity within him, which he could draw upon at any time if he would just decide to do it. Or more precisely, if one does not choose (when there are alternative possibilities within or before him), it is because he has *chosen* not to choose. His incapacity to choose is willfully and freely determined, not fixed or fatal. The retreat from choice is a choice in itself.

I am not prepared to consent that a human being can *hopelessly* destroy himself. If there is any evidence that a human being can become totally and irretrievably psychopathic, I have yet to see it. If the fact that few or no psychopaths have ever been cured or helped is cited as evidence, then I should counter that I know few, if any, psychologists whose character and personality are beautiful and wise enough to entice a psychopath to see any value or reason in changing his attitude. I can say earnestly that I know too many psychologists who give up too easily, not to mention those who are virtually devoid of genuine and profound care for their patients. I doubt that any person can make himself such a complete coward or become so neurotic or psychotic that he becomes a *total* automaton, directed only by blind impulses and conditioned reaction formations over which he has not the slightest degree of free control.

In this regard, I share the view of Viktor Frankl, the renowned Austrian logotherapist. In *Man's Search for Meaning,* Dr. Frankl says:

. . . a human being is a finite being, and his freedom is restricted. It is not freedom from conditions, but freedom to take a stand toward the conditions. . . .Man is *not* fully conditioned and determined; he determines himself whether to give in to conditions or stand up to them. In other words, man is ultimately self-determining. Man does not simply exist, but always decides what his existence will be, what he will become in the next moment. . . . *every human being has the freedom to change at any instant.* Therefore, we can predict his future only within the large frame of a statistical survey referring to a whole group; the individual personality, however, remains essentially unpredictable.[2]

With such a limited quotation here, it is possible that I may give a misleading impression of Dr. Frankl's view of human nature. He does not subscribe to the existentialist view of Sartre that man has no essential nature, nor do I. According to Sartre, a person is born as a "free" being, and this means that he is without any essences to qualify, limit, or determine his nature. Man first must "exist"; only later can he determine his own essences by "free choice," whereby he makes himself what he is. In the beginning, man is a "being without essence," which means that he is *nothing;* or rather, he is influenced by nothing, caused by nothing, explained by nothing. To exist freely, a person must come into being totally uncaused, created by nothing. According to Sartre, that which exists necessarily, or is in any way determined to be what it is, cannot exist freely. A human being is "nothing" until he acts, until he "makes himself" what he is. And since he is determined by absolutely nothing, he is "absolutely free." Consequently, he is "absolutely responsible" for all that he is and does.

If we ask Sartre what he means by his phrase "existence precedes essence," he answers:

It means that, first of all, man exists, turns up, appears on the scene, and, only afterwards, defines himself. If man, as the existentialist conceives him, is indefinable, it is because at first he is *nothing.* Only afterward will he be something, and he himself will have made what he will be. . . . Not only is man what he conceives himself to be, but he is also only what he wills himself to be after this *thrust toward existence.*

Man is nothing else but what he makes of himself.[3]

Here, after considerable laborious effort to understand Sartre, I must confess that I fail to make any sense of him at all. Either he possesses some esoteric insight into man and his freedom, and I am too obtuse to share it, or there is something essentially nonsensical in his attempt to ground man and his freedom in nothingness. I must agree with his clear implication, on the one hand, that a human being is an agent responsible for his choices between alternative possibilities for acting. Half of the time, Sartre talks as though a person is a spiritual agent, and his capacity to choose is one of the *essences* of his nature. Indeed, in a variety of essays he argues that a human being is free even when he chooses not to be free. Freedom, he says, is *necessary* because it is essentially impossible for anyone to escape it, except in death.

On the other hand, however, Sartre unwittingly thwarts his own position by implying that no one can really make his own choices. All my life I have been accustomed to thinking that choices are made by existing *agents*. A person sees alternative possibilities for action, then he acts on one of them, and his action thus constitutes his choice. In other words, there can be no choice except when there is a free agent to make it. It is the agent himself who is responsible for the choice because it is he, and he only, who makes it. Freedom is grounded essentially in the capacity of an agent to act on alternative possibilities, and in his awareness of this capacity. A person is only as free as how many possibilities he has to act on. Also, he is only as free as the ones he *chooses* to act on. In short, if there is no agent with alternative possibilities for action, then there is no freedom of choice at all. I find it inconceivable that a choice can be made by "nothing," that only "nothingness" is free. One of my colleagues, a disciple of Sartre, insists that he has "chosen to be born." I myself know of no choices except those that are made by individual agents. How anyone could choose to be born before first existing with a capacity to choose strains my understanding to infinity.

Sartre is a phenomenologist, of the noncausal sort: he looks upon the mind not as an agent but as a stream of consciousness which comes out of nothing. There is no mind, as a spirit or soul. There is only a stream of images, sensations, perceptions, ideas, concepts, feelings, and volitions. Each of these mental phenomena is uncaused, for it is created by "nothing." This stream of consciousness (which people ordinarily regard as occurring in some mind, and as belonging to some person) actually belongs to nobody at all. For while, on the one hand, Sartre insists on man's freedom to determine his own conscious states, on the other, he defines consciousness as something that simply happens, without any possible ontological basis or explanation. As for the source of consciousness, or the conditions which make thought possible, he insists that, in the final analysis, there are no conditions and no source whatever. On the contrary, if thought were produced by an agent (i.e., a being essentially spiritual in nature), this would mean that we are born with essences; this, in turn, would mean that we are bound by some inborn qualities that limit our freedom. According to Sartre, we must at all cost avoid believing in anything that would limit our freedom to determine our own essences. It is for this reason that we must reject the idea of God and the soul. If man were born as a soul (i.e., in essence a spirit), he would be shackled by his inherited nature. If a human being had an immortal soul, he would be enslaved by his own essences, simply because he could not choose to end his own life in death. If God existed, he would determine the basic essences of man. He would determine the limits of man and the values by which we ought to live. Consequently, we would be basically determined by him rather than totally determined by ourselves, which would make us his slaves. For this reason, we should reject God as a cumbersome myth—he simply would be a hindrance to our freedom.

According to Sartre, the ultimate source of consciousness is an "impersonal spontaneity." Consciousness, we are told, "determines its existence at each instant, without our being able to conceive anything *before* it. Thus each instant of our conscious life reveals to us a creation *ex nihilo*. . . .There is something distressing for each of us, to catch in the act this tireless creation of existence of which *we* are not the creators."[4]

In these remarks, Sartre seems to affirm the existence of a "spontaneity" which transcends freedom, if by freedom we mean a person's *capacity* for self-determination. I certainly do agree with him that there is something "distressing" in this doctrine if he means, as he appears to, that the spontaneity he is affirming is not anyone's spontaneity, but rather is some mystical nothingness belonging to nobody or not a part of anybody. As a matter of fact, he seems to be presenting in disguise the determinism of Nietzsche, the nihilist who insisted that we are totally controlled by something transcending all of us. Echoing the blind will of Schopenhauer, Nietzsche says, fatalistically: "A thought comes when 'it' will and not when 'I' will. It is thus a *falsification* of the evidence to say that the subject 'I' conditions the predicate 'think.' "[5]

Sartre often has pleaded passionately for the "authentic existence" of the individual person. To my knowledge, he has more than any other philosopher stressed and restressed the reality and moral necessity for man's self-determination. I know of no one who has more greatly emphasized man's need for independence and a sense of responsibility in making his own free choices. Nevertheless, the question is: Does not Sartre, in effect, end by reducing the individual agent to a nonentity or a mere product, in the same way that the relativists and behaviorists have done? For clearly, he denies that a man can create his own conscious states. We must remember that he says of consciousness: "There is something distressing for each of us, to catch in the act this tireless creation of which *we are not the creators.*"

If I correctly read Sartre (and I have read him over and over), I must protest what he has done to my personal autonomy. Or more exactly, I must revolt against his theory because, if it were true, I could enjoy no real autonomy whatever. Sartre takes the spontaneity or freedom that properly belongs to me and transfers it to a transcendent nothingness, then absurdly assigns to it the responsibility for all my choices. If all choices are made by "nothingness," then they certainly are not made by me, and I neither can nor shall assume any responsibility for them. I think even a child would ask (in his superior common sense): "How can *nothingness* choose?" How can there be an act of creation without a creator, or a choice without a person or creature to do the choosing? How can there be freedom without an agent who is free? While insisting that every individual is absolutely free, Sartre in no way clarifies how or in what way freedom is a part of the individual's nature. In short, he deprives freedom of any meaningful ontological basis of intelligibility. His freedom enjoys the absurdity of being neither a subject nor an object, neither a quality nor a principle, neither a capacity nor a fact. It is simply the spontaneous and impersonal happening of the data of consciousness *out of nothing*.

What I cannot grasp is how a meaningful and valuable experience could come out of totally meaningless and valueless nothingness. Sartre never really faces this question. He makes no effort to explain this position, except to say: he who holds that both being and nothingness ultimately are absurd is categorically an atheist. Sartre himself grants that his theory is unintelligible —or rather, that it is only as intelligible as anyone should expect in an irrational world. However, there can be no gainsaying the inconsistency of this position. It simply makes no sense to present the world's unintelligibility as a rational assumption. There can be no *rational* evidence that all existence is per se irrational. For obviously, irrationality or absurdity can be known as such only from the standpoint of some rational person. If existence were categorically irrational (which Sartre presumes to be the case), then how could it produce rational persons who have a knowledge of such a fact?

Sartre is, in fact, quite unaware of the arbitrary character of his atheism. He attributes belief in God entirely to naïveté and wishful thinking. He regards atheism as an intellectual necessity and believes a person can exist authentically only if he banishes his faith in God and the soul.

Here I wish to return to the pragmatic tenet of my earlier concern, namely, that all our judgments are arbitrary, uncertain, and fallible. On this point, the pragmatists enjoy the complete support of the Sartrian nihilists. Actually, both schools attack each other as irrational, for each regards its position as different and true. Nonetheless, both theoretically deny that anyone can have a knowledge of objective truths. For example, the pragmatists accuse the existentialists of being "unscientific," and the Sartrians, whose numbers are greater than is commonly known, consider pragmatists to be tyrants in disguise. Existentialists charge pragmatists with browbeating man with science, and with drowning the individual in the social whole.

I certainly would concur with this charge. However, it is a bit incredible that the Sartrian can make such an accusation, yet be totally blind to essentially the same fault in his own theory. Pragmatism clearly denies that a human being *is* a human being, that he *owns* the essences of humanness. Existentialism throws all essences to the winds; therefore, it cannot rightfully complain against the pragmatist for doing the same. Both Sartre and Dewey deny that there is any objective stature to moral values and logic. Both theoretically turn a human being into a product of some impersonal force, although neither is aware of it nor has ever admitted it. What both have in common is an intellectual schizophrenia: they demand in practice a respect for objective truths and values which in theory they deny.

If man has no essential humanness, as both of these philosophers insist, then an intelligible philosophy of autonomy is categorically hopeless. It takes no little patience to read Dewey's renunciations of essential truths, then to bear with his preachments that all of us *ought* to seek goodness and truth and live by it. It is no less easy to endure the statements of Sartre, who tells us that existence is futile. Unfortunately, many other people believe this, and they turn from life altogether or become neurotic and dissipate thoroughly. Whereupon, Sartre accuses them of behaving "inauthentically," of abusing their possibilities for growth in self-meaning. One can easily ask him: What point is there in suffering the pains of integrity if *all* of life is essentially pointless? Why struggle against the futility of a life which, by definition, would make all struggle essentially in vain?

I find little unity in the thinking of this philosopher. At the bottom of page 615 in *Being and Nothingness,* he says, "A human being is a useless passion." Speaking through the first person in his novel *Nausea,* he says, " . . . here we sit, all of us, eating and drinking to preserve our precious existence and really there is nothing, nothing, absolutely no reason for existing."[6] Then later: "Every existing thing is born without reason, prolongs itself out of weakness and dies by chance."[7] Although he is speaking here through a novel, it is obvious that he is dramatizing an attitude that is properly his own. It seems that Sartre's contradiction lies primarily in his inability either to truly renounce life or truly affirm it. Were we to listen to the voice of Sartre's theory, we should commit suicide, on the grounds that life is not really worth living. But then, if we followed him in practice, we would deeply engross ourselves in life; we would discover, and live by, abiding values and truths which are essential to our identity and integrity as persons.

In *Nausea,* Sartre says:

The essential thing is contingency. I mean that one cannot define existence as necessity. To exist is simply *to be there;* those who exist let themselves be encountered, but you can never deduce anything from them. I believe there are people who have understood this. Only they tried to overcome this contingency by inventing a necessary, causal being (God). But no necessary being can explain existence: contingency is not a delusion, a probability which can be dissipated; it is the *absolute,* consequently, the perfect free gift.[8]

If one takes the above remarks in the full context of Sartre's writings, their meaning becomes unmistakably clear. The French atheist means to say that there is only one absolute truth, namely, that everything in life occurs purely by happenstance, for there are no necessary truths, values, facts, or meanings. There is no reason for anything whatever to exist. Nothing in life is essential. There are no necessities, no abiding essences.

At this point, the pragmatist and existentialist join hands in theory. According to pragmatist Lawrence Thomas, reality "consists ultimately not of terms or essences as self-contained existents, but of relationships or processes, which constitute and exhaust the meanings of things or essences."[9] Thus, while Sartre reduces the realities of life ultimately to nothing, Thomas reduces them to a "process," which is itself meaningless except from the standpoint of life's "terms" or "essences"—which he declares to be unreal. In Sartre, we are caught up in categorical meaninglessness. In hopeless contradiction, we seek meanings in a world where no essential meanings can exist or abide. In Thomas, we revolve in a giddy, vicious circle. We locate the meanings of process only in essences, which we declare to be illusions. Simultaneously, we locate the meanings of life's essences only in process, which without essences also is meaningless and unreal.

As a religious realist, I could not pretend to be able to explain essences. I only know that there are essences, that there are realities which essentially *are* what they *are*. Certainly, I leave it to the Lord to *explain* the essences of things. I do not have to be able to explain any essences in order to be able to recognize them. I simply know that essences are what make identity and recognition possible. It is impossible to identify anything definite, or to distinguish one reality from another, if there are no essences, if nothing *is* essentially what it *is*. When I divorce essences from being, I end up with no being at all. When I extract all the essences from an apple, I end up without any apple whatever. I cannot conceive of any being that is not, in essence, what it is; nor can I conceive of how knowledge or experience is possible if there are no essences whereby meaningful distinctions in reality can be made. Without essences, I cannot imagine how any person can distinguish between himself and other persons or things. I cannot imagine how any person can talk intelligibly about any definite realities or facts.

Sartre speaks of our "thrust toward existence," asking us to believe that it is "nothingness" which thrusts us into being, thereby creating our lives. Such muddy reasoning as this cannot satisfy the intellectual needs of a child, much less those of a rational adult. Searching for truth in Sartre, we come to the same dead end wherever we turn, namely, to *nothingness*. Man is essentially nothing. Both in Dewey and in Sartre we inevitably drown.

As a realist, I cannot deny the pragmatic belief in a process, but I insist on making process meaningful, which cannot be done except by dealing with essences. Even a process (the action whereby essences ingress into and out of different subjects and objects) must be *essentially* a process, or else there is no process at all. Whatever a process is, it *is* essentially what it *is*. No day will come when human beings will be able to explain the process of life. God must exist to explain it, or it is absurd, as Sartre claims. But if it is absurd, we unmistakably are doomed.

For certainly, no values and meanings can be conserved in a world where everything is contingent and nothing is essential.

Neither pragmatism nor existentialism has any cogent grounds upon which to stand. Indeed the contrary is true—both of these doctrines make any objective criteria of philosophical cogency theoretically impossible. First, they tell us that there are no laws of logic. Then, they tell us that there are no objective moral values. What they are really telling us is that there is no way of reasoning that is *in essence* any more rational or less rational than any other way of reasoning. Nor is there any way of acting that is in essence any more moral or immoral than any other way of acting. No motive can be essentially any better or worse than any other motive. In the arts, no performance is in essence any more or less artistic than any other. But the pragmatists, and their existentialist first cousins, have yet to suggest how meaningful distinctions can be made if there are no essences in the world. They take satisfaction in throwing out the essences of truth, beauty, and goodness; but how truth, beauty, and goodness are possible without essences, they deign not to consider.

In behalf of my case in this book, I have to appeal ultimately to common sense. We play havoc with commonsense knowledge when we deny that morality requires some *essential* values and principles. If there is no person whose character is, in essence, any more or less autonomous than any other's, then obviously it is pointless to strive after an intelligible philosophy and psychology of individual autonomy. We must presuppose that human beings have essences, a *humanness* in common. We have some definite needs and traits in common, without which there could be no foundation for social authority, nor for a rational social psychology. In addition to this, we must honor the *unique* needs and traits essential only to the individual, without which there could be no self-authority and no individual psychology.

All of us have the following essences in common as human beings:

1. The capacity to make choices between alternative possibilities for action (our freedom of decision).

2. The capacity to know, to distinguish ourselves from other persons, creatures, and things through experience.
3. The capacity for self-reflection and self-evaluation.
4. The capacity for self-deception, self-neglect, and self-alienation.
5. The capacity for self-detachment, humor, laughter, and self-transcendence.
6. The capacity to create, to act on possibilities and transform them into concrete realities.
7. The capacity to experience related meanings and values, to unify and organize the data of consciousness.

There are, of course, other essences in human nature, but it is not a part of my purpose to tally them in fine detail in this book. Also, I should readily acknowledge (indeed, insist) that the presence of these capacities varies in degree from person to person, according to each one's heredity. Moreover, I should accord that these capacities cannot manifest themselves where there is no environmental opportunity for them to do so. A person's hereditary talent may be locked up in an environmental prison. In some isolated tribe, for example, some child may be born as a potential mathematical genius but be limited or held down by the most primitive cultural conditions. This could mean that he may never learn to multiply even the simplest numbers, simply because he has no chance to learn.

A viable doctrine of autonomy must look at the individual's life from the standpoint of two factors, namely, (1) his essential capacities or potentialities, and (2) the opportunities that he and his society can provide each other for the development of their talents in constructive ways.

A pragmatic or existentialist philosophy cannot serve as a basis for both individual and social autonomy. We inevitably do violence to ourselves when we try to freewheel through the world as though it has no essential laws, facts, truths, and values. We must search for, discover, and honor that nature that is *essential* in each human being and in need of development. Theoretically, pragmatism and existentialism deny essences categorically. It would follow logically from their doctrine that there is nothing essential in, to, or for any human being's life. Dewey and Sartre reduce morality to nothing more than personal power, preference, and taste, which are wholly arbitrary and subjective. However, they do this only in theory, very inconsistently, and without ever really acknowledging it. In practice, both have often objected to the conduct of many people as "unreasonable" and "immoral." The critical question is: On what grounds can they complain, after they have thrown out all the world's *essential* moral and logical principles?

In the real world, no degree of sanity and autonomy is possible unless true knowledge is possible. By true knowledge, I mean an awareness of the facts, laws, capacities, and ideals essential to man and the universe in which we live. The individual must acquire a knowledge of his own *essential* nature. He can afford to have no illusions about that which it is necessary for him to do if he is to fulfill his life. He must come to know what his essential needs are. He must learn his essential limitations and capabilities. And what is extremely important, he must learn to recognize and honor the essential logic of human rights; for it is only in a society where this is done that he can be safeguarded from the arbitrary actions of evil and irrational persons with power. Bogged down in the quicksand of relativism, the pragmatist can have no future in his arbitrariness and doubt. No knowledge of man's essential nature and needs can be founded in doubt. Doubt never builds anything. No facts can be founded in it. No hope can reside in it. No joy can thrive on it.

If I were a relativist, I would despair of ever finding *any* truths if I complied with my original premise that truth can be found only in the whole. As I mentioned earlier, relativism insists that all things are mutually and reciprocally determined. The part can have no reality except in the whole. When anything is changed, everything in the universe is changed. And since everything is constantly changing, nothing can ever *be* what it *is*. Since I cannot know the whole, I cannot know anything for certain. Thus, I would despair.

This, I submit, is the arbitrariness of the useless doctrine that all human judgments are merely arbitrary.

At the banquet of a philosophical conference I once attended, I found myself seated beside a pragmatist who insisted that nothing can be known for certain. It happened that I was a fast eater and he was a slow eater. Upon finishing my own pie, I took his and began to eat it. Fortunately, as I had hoped, he saw me do it out of the corner of his eye. Whereupon, he complained, "Just who in the hell do you think you are?" And I said, "Well, sir, aren't you yourself being just a bit presumptuous? I mean, you are accusing me of stealing your pie, when you cannot be at all certain that it was I who took it. In fact, how do you *know* for certain that there was ever a piece of pie on the table?" He answered, "You know damn well you took my pie! Just what are you trying to prove?" I said, "I am merely trying to prove that your pragmatic dogma of uncertainty is unreal. If you will simply admit that you know for *certain* that you exist, that we are in a banquet room together, and that definite knowledge of reality is possible, than I shall happily go to a bakery and buy you a whole pie. But if you are still uncertain that you exist, then you must also be uncertain that I stole your dessert."

4.

Private Knowledge:
"A Contradiction in Terms"

BEFORE presenting my principles of autonomy, I must attempt to refute more of the principles of pragmatism. In this chapter, I shall attack several tenets of this popular doctrine which I find preoccupied with unhealthy compromises and social adjustment. I regard all the tenets of pragmatism to be inimical to moral integrity and to rational reason.

I have already accused relativism of reducing reality to a jungle of ambiguities and contradictions. To a realist, this doctrine seems continuously to spite its own premises and to refute its own terms. Pragmatism turns the world into a rash of paralogisms in which no knowledge of objective and logical realities would be possible. First, it insists that all truth varies from individual to individual; but then, it says that, as individuals, we can know no truth at all because no individual can have his own private truth or knowledge. We are first told that all truths are only individual or relative. But then, we are told that there is no truth except that which is social. For example, I have quoted Arnstine as saying, "All the perceptions, feelings, and thoughts a person has are relative to him." As a realist, I definitely agree with this, and I insist that I can know what most of my own perceptions are. At least I am usually aware of the things that happen in my mind on the conscious level; that is, I perceive things around me and *know* that I perceive them. I perceive a red apple on a green table against a yellow wall, and *know* that I perceive all these things.

Unfortunately, however, Mr. Arnstine goes on to insist that my perceptions are not really mine at all. He says that they do not "belong" to me, for there can be no such things as individual minds or agents which think. I cannot have my own private perceptions and know that I have them. Arnstine attempts to defend the dogmatic tenet of pragmatism that *no knowledge is legitimate except that which can be scientifically demonstrated or publicly verified.* If this were true, I would have to reject most of my knowledge of reality since it is grounded in my private history of perceptions and experiences, i.e., experiences that only *I* have had. For example, on a certain morning when I had breakfast alone I ate three eggs and three slices of bacon, and drank a glass of orange juice. I also took a shower bath, and no one saw me do this. In the case of my breakfast, I ate the evidence; and in the case of my shower, the evidence dried up or went down the drain. It is hardly feasible that I could *publicly* verify taking my bath, at least not by pragmatism's criterion of knowledge, which is social sharing and agreement of observation. I am scarcely prone to allow the public to watch me bathe. According to pragmatism, no person can have his own private feelings, perceptions, and thoughts and *know* through his intuition that his private experiences are his own and are real.

Mr. Arnstine declares that all knowledge

is always relative to some group. . . .

Knowing something is, of course, different from perceiving, feeling, or merely thinking something. Because knowledge appears to make some claim to being objective, it is often assumed that perceptions, feelings, and thoughts are merely subjective. . . .Indeed, knowledge has a public status not so easily achieved by other kinds of *so-called* mental events. . . .What we know, then—or what we *think* we know—consists of those of our perceptions that have undergone some *test,* and that, consequently have been found to be *similar to the perceptions of others.* This is to say that we do not directly (through our own individual perceptions) know anything at all.[1]

Quoad hoc, personal autonomy is impossible because individual knowledge is unreal.

This brings us to another of pragmatism's tenets, that *the criterion of truth is agreement among scientific observers.* This means: unless I can *test* what I have seen and done, and unless I allow the scientific public to test it also, I can have no legitimate right to think that I have really seen it or done it. Within this framework of pragmatism there can be no private knowledge. There can be no grasp of objective truth except when one's perceptions are "similar to the perceptions of others." This inevitably restricts individual wisdom or knowledge to the prevailing opinions and attitudes of the group. And of course, the group is truly wise only if it is made up at large of scientists.

Earlier, I referred to John Dewey's objection to the notion of private experience. It is necessary to repeat this passage for present purposes.

. . . one can hardly use the term "experience" in philosophical discourse, but a critic rises to inquire "Whose experience?" The question is asked in *adverse criticism.* Its implication is that experience by its very nature is owned by some one; and that the ownership is such in kind that everything about experience is affected by a private and exclusive quality.[2]

I readily agree that this criticism is "adverse." For I have no knowledge of any experience that does not belong to some particular individual and is not in some respects exclusive and private. I know, for example, that no other person on earth knows me as I know myself. I have had innumerable experiences when I was alone, which I cannot possibly retrieve to share with other persons under identical circumstances. Moreover, even if it were possible to do this, the experiences would be new to the others while they would be repetitions to me, which is different. The unique, personal love that I feel for my wife certainly is an experience which I, and only I, can have in this way. If I have this special joy (which is special for the very reason that it is uniquely mine—unduplicable in, by, or for other persons), is this not a legitimate part of my knowledge of reality? Is it not legitimate knowledge simply because I cannot explain it to the public, or submit it to a group of scientists who would dissect, analyze, measure, and classify it?

Dewey complains that "the implication is that experience by its very nature is *owned* by someone."

If I have an ache in my back, am I really to believe that it does not hurt *me*? Is Dewey asking me to believe that my backache is a *public* experience, belonging to no one, and that my experience of it has no private and exclusive quality? Does the back just experience its own ache, and is there no particular person who uniquely feels and laments it, as no one but *I* can?

We could hush the pragmatist simply by challenging him to present a single experience that does not belong to somebody. However, let us listen to Dewey further, so that we may see better into the workings of his pragmatic mind. He proceeds to tell us that this "implication is as absurd as it would be to infer from the fact that houses are usually owned, are mine and yours and his, that possessive reference so permeates the properties of being a house that nothing intelligible can be said about the latter."[3]

In other words, Dewey is telling us that there is no difference between a house and a person's experience of a house. As one would expect from a pragmatist, I find in Dewey's logic no distinction between a subject and an object, between the object of experience and the subject who has the experience. In short, there is no difference between the knower and the known. Dewey insists that experience "recognizes in its primary integrity no division between act and material, subject and object, but contains them both in an *unanalyzed totality*."[4]

If this were true, should we not conclude from it that something exists as an object in reality if it exists only as an image or idea in someone's thought? Since Dewey allows no distinction between a house and an experience of a house, does he offer some means to distinguish between real knowledge about houses and mere illusions about houses? Dewey does in fact recognize the gravity of this problem, and he offers his own definition of objective truth, with what he considers an adequate means to distinguish between mere subjective belief and objective knowledge. No less than a realist, the pragmatist insists on some method of distinguishing between truth and falsehood, fact and fiction, despite his dogma of universal uncertainty! This distinction is summed up briefly by his disciple Lawrence Thomas, who reduces objectivity simply to social consensus. Thomas says that "the meaning of objectivity" is lost as long as we regard it as the "revelation of what is actually 'out there.' " Since nothing can exist outside of human experience, objectivity must be regarded as "agreement amongst observers on the content of their shared experiences—i.e., objectivity means inter-subjective corroboration."[5]

Thus, it is evident that pragmatists are never consistent with their premises of relativism and scepticism, since they too insist on a method of distinguishing between true and false beliefs. Nonetheless, they have not the slightest understanding of the need for rational consistency in the conception of truth. A pragmatist has yet to admit that he exists in a real world where other individuals and things exist apart from him but can be known. In Dewey's theory of knowledge, there are no realities existing independently of our thought. We do not *discover* truth; we "make" it. We do not discover the objects of knowledge; we "achieve" them. This now brings us to another tenet of pragmatism, namely, that *all truths are man-made.*

Another disciple of Dewey, Frederick Neff, tells us that "so-called extra mundane truths are reducible to human judgment and human interpretation . . . *truth is neither more nor less than what man assesses it to be.*"[6] In *Philosophy and Civilization,* Dewey treats all past history as though it has no reality except in thought, and he reduces truth solely to the phenomena of immediate experience. He says, "Pragmatism . . . presents itself as an extension of historical empiricism (scientism), but with this fundamental difference, that it does not insist upon *antecedent* phenomena. . . ."[7] From here, he goes on to tell us that science or knowledge is never based "upon antecedent phenomena," nor "upon the precedents," but rather "upon the possibilities of action."[8] A realist can hardly help being mystified by this notion, that we live in a world of real possibilities, but in a world with no past. By no stretch of my mental capacities can I conceive of a real today without a real yesterday; nor can I conceive of a tomorrow which will not rest in some basic respects upon the antecedent truths of today.

In this matter, however, Dewey is not at all consistent. In his writings in general he unmistakably shows a belief in a real past, and he insists on the reality of evolution. For example, in *Human Nature and Conduct,* he speaks of "habits" as though they definitely are rooted in a real past from which they are carried over, etc. Nowhere in his writings does he attempt to explain how there can be present possibilities for action if there is no actual past which also was not laden with possibilities. That there can be a real present without a real past is utterly unimaginable. Nonetheless, Dewey blinds himself to this simple fact; for otherwise, he could not adhere to his dogma that all truths are man-made. As a realist, I must insist that I have *discovered* the Rocky Mountains, and that I was able to do so only because they actually existed in objective reality *before* I came upon them. In other words, I did not invent them, or "forge" them, or "achieve" them, as the pragmatists say. I was able to have an experience of them only because they were there, with both a present and a past existence of their own, independently of my experience of them. But of course, I could never convince a pragmatist of this.

According to Neff, "truth 'emerges' from the testing of hypotheses, which is to say that it is *not antecedent* to investigation."[9] In other words, the Rocky Mountains did not exist before I investigated them. Or to be yet more pragmatic, they never existed before some scientifically oriented scholars established a hypothesis to that effect and then proceeded to test it. Of course, even a child would be repulsed by this. He would ask the pragmatist: "How can you investigate anything at all if there are no antecedent realities which are the objects of your investigation?" But then Neff would answer, true to expectations: "Instead of being discovered, truth is *formulated, constructed,* or *brought into being.* The act of inquiry 'yields' truth—it does not merely 'come upon' it as a preformed entity . . . . Rather, it means that man 'forges' truth out of the responsible process of careful investigation of evidence."[10]

I cannot take this seriously. Just how *un*realistic can professional philosophers become?

Unfortunately, it is possible for students in our colleges to grow progressively more intellectually lost as they acquire more and more degrees. Generally, pragmatism is propagated by "doctors." These sages live on the twentieth floor of the ivory tower and never descend. Obviously, they entice many innocent dupes into their parlors, wine them on the moonshine of sophistry, and turn them into zealous disciples. It is a notable fact, however, that they make converts only of irrational adults and adolescents; for children, dogs, and cats are realists throughout —they can by no means or legerdemain be deceived into thinking that the objects around them do not really exist. To any child, and to any animal, the earth is the earth and the sky is the sky. Nobody with good sense can be enticed to believe that men "forge" the existence of the oceans, the galaxies, and the cosmos. The pragmatic hoax reaches into the minds of only the simple. And I mean not the profoundly simple, but those who would turn the simple truth into a bewildering and preposterous complexity or confusion.

What can Neff possibly mean when he insists that we do not "come upon" the Rocky Mountains? If he means that they do not exist except in our minds, he is reducing knowledge to solipsism and obscuring it beyond repair. How can we make a "careful investigation of evidence" if evidence has no existence except in what we invent in our minds? Does he not clearly state that there is no reality except what we "forge," "formulate," and "bring into being"? Starting with this premise, would it not follow that all evidence itself is nothing except what we bring into being? Also, would it not follow that no evidence can be investigated until we first "construct" it in order that we can then investigate it? This is an extremely self-contradictory idea of the nature of truth. For first, we must "construct" a hypothesis which refers to no reality at all except to that which we "construct." Then, we must construct a "test" which actually can test nothing except that which we construct to be tested. Finally, we "bring into being" a truth which never existed before we invented it and fabricated the evidence to "test" it. The Rocky Mountains are the Rocky Mountains only after we construct them; or more pragmatically yet, they are so only after we have constructed a test of the construction of our construction. When an outdoorsman goes camping on the Cache la Poudre, the trees and rapids cease to exist after he pitches a tent, crawls into his sleeping bag, and falls asleep.

Pragmatic defenses of this absurd position rest entirely in John Dewey's doctrine of experience as something that is impersonal. As I mentioned earlier, Dewey regards experience as just a "doing and an undergoing," as nothing more than a series of impersonal happenings. Defending this view of Dewey's, Thomas tells us:

> The phrase "doing and undergoing" directs attention to the subjective features of experience. It is the subject who is doing and undergoing. The objects in his experience are the products of his doing and undergoing. His experience does not discover or disclose objects *antecedently* given. Rather, his experience *achieves* objects by differentiation and abstraction, through the cycle of doing and undergoing.[11]

For a moment, Thomas almost gives the impression that he, too, distinguishes between subject and object, between the thing experienced and the person who has the experience. He verges upon the commonsense understanding that experience always belongs to somebody. But unfortunately, this would be just too rational to expect from a pragmatist. Shortly following, he adds: "Something of the ultimate nature of subjects and objects has already been indicated. They are *twin-born* in the differentiating transaction of on-going experience."[12]

Now here, I am left whirling on the outer edge of the great Vicious Circle. First, Dewey and his disciples tell me that I do not exist as a real agent who owns his own experiences. On the contrary (I am told), experience is impersonal and *it owns me,* not I it. Dewey says that "candid regard for scientific inquiry" compels me to recognize that "when experience does occur, no matter at what limited portion of time and space, it enters into possession of some portion of nature and in such a manner as to render other of its precincts accessible."[13]

Then, he proceeds to explain that experience "enters into possession" of me; it is not I who possess it. Under Dewey's ontology, I end up as an object of some impersonal "doing and undergoing." Experience "enters into possession of . . . nature" in order to "render . . . its precincts accessible."

To escape drowning here, I have to thrust my head out of the pragmatic waters—I cry out, "Accessible to *whom*?! Accessible to me?!"

Pragmatically speaking, I have not discovered myself as a subject, nor discovered the objects existing around me. On the contrary, myself and the objects are "achieved" by some "doing and undergoing," which is an impersonal process over which I have not the slightest control. Both myself and the world of others are "achieved" by "experience," which is something that just "occurs, happens, and is what it is."[14] In short, the human being does not *exist,* nor does he *discover* anything in the world surrounding him. The objects of his experience simply have no antecedent reality; they just come into being at the same time that he comes into being, and both are one and the same thing. In fact, all seemingly separate and distinct subjects and objects in the world are really one and the same thing. Reality unifies all subjects and objects into one "unanalyzable totality." If I may once again cite the testimony of the master: "Experience recognizes in its primary integrity no division between act and material, subject and object, but contains them both in an *unanalyzable totality.*"[15] Here, there seem to be absurdities piling upon absurdities.

As Neff has pointed out, the pragmatist does not wish to be associated with the nihilist. He does not want it thought that the doctrine which says man makes all truth means that all ideas are true, or that "wishing will make it so."[16] In an attempt to escape his dilemma, Neff resorts to Dewey's "transaction" doctrine that knowledge is an interaction or "transaction" between the "knowing and the known." Dewey insists that knowledge is the result of a transaction between the individual and his environment. In attempting to defend this view, his disciples fail to see the essential stupidity in making knowledge the result of a transaction after they have analyzed away the terms between which real transactions might occur. After the fashion of Arnstine, Neff says that realism

has traditionally viewed the senses as a means of bridging the gap between the knower and the objects of knowledge, whereas pragmatism views perception, not as a series of discrete acts, but as an interaction that *includes* both percipient organisms and things *said* to be perceived. It is understood as a unitary relationship wherein the whole "field" is engaged. . . .Perhaps the possibility of misconstruction led Dewey to prefer the term "transaction," for he was concerned with preserving what might be called the "integrity" of the total human situation by not cutting it off from its environing conditions. The wholeness of things Dewey prized more highly than their separateness, not only in respect to the transactional relationship between knowing and the known, but also in regard to the integration of knowledge through the continuous reconstruction of experience.[17]

Hard as he tries to add clarity to Dewey's relativism, Neff succeeds only in propagating the already sufficient noise and confusion on the pragmatist scene. For in what way can he help the "integrity" of the "total human situation" by not "cutting it off from its environing conditions"? Being "cut off" from his environment is precisely the first demand every person must make if he is to succeed in really being an individual. In simple truth, there can be no human integrity whatever except in the *separate* and *distinct* individual who is both logically and existentially discontinuous from other individuals and things. Of course individuals exist in a world, in an environment, and they are related to one another. But there is no possible way to imagine individuals existing in a relationship of any kind if they are unreal as *individual beings*. We must ask Neff the same question we put to all relativists: If your "whole field" is a pure continuum (an absolute unity of being in which there are no separate or discontinuous beings with individual integrity), then between whom, or between what, can your so-called transaction take place?

This world I live in is no "unanalyzable totality." It is no "pure continuum," no meaningless one. Reality is a pluralistic and analyzable variety of different persons, creatures, and objects, or it is nothing.

Pragmatism offers two more tenets that the autonomous individual must categorically reject. They are: *Reality is a pure continuum,* and *reality is experience.* The former needs no sophisticated argument to be proved wrong. This dogma will be laughed out of the court of common sense, for we cannot help distinguishing one person from another while we remain sane. I am not you, and you are not me. Our beings are different and separate. I am I, and you are you, only because each of us is a unique agent who is discontinuous from the other. The notion that all subjects and objects are continuous with each other (continue into and constitute each other) is incredibly senseless. Did anyone ever try to drive a nail with a hammer continuous with the board?

The proposition that "experience is reality" is equally witless. This is but a gross oversimplification which fails to distinguish between experience and the things that are experienced. Were this pragmatic dogma true, I would find myself inseparable from the table on which I am writing, the pen I hold in my hand, and all the things that exist around me. When I hang my coat in the closet, I do precisely that—I hang my coat in the closet; I do not hang up an experience. I have not left an experience parked in my garage; I have left my car there. I have an experience of the chair I am sitting in; it does not have an experience of me, and it is not an experience.

There is scarcely a single pragmatic principle upon which personal autonomy can thrive. In fact, this entire doctrine is anathema to the spirit of individual reality and worth. The pseudoscientific tenet that *all conclusions should be tentative* is but another of pragmatism's self-contradictory absolutes. Like the others, this dogma is a dangerous oversimplification; it is an attempt to reduce all the meanings and realities of our life to a merely scientific undertaking. I believe it is a perfectly reasonable assumption that a scientist, as scientist, should hold tentative conclusions while his hypotheses are unproved, or are susceptible to a reasonable doubt. In the presence of inconclusive evidence, no one has a right to call himself a scientist if he dogmatizes about purely scientific matters while faking experiments or ignoring relevant facts. However, no human being is ever only a scientist. All of us live in a world in which moral, artistic, and religious problems are just as real as scientific or technological problems.

For example, as long as a human being is alive and conscious he has responsibilities both to himself and to others. From the standpoint of morality, this is a conclusion that no person can ever afford to lay aside. That I have real responsibilities is a conclusion which I must hold to permanently; for otherwise, the moment I decide I have no responsibility I become psychopathic or insensitive, and I endanger both my own well-being and that of others. On moral grounds, the court must outlaw the baleful dogma that a human being has no right to persevere in any of his convictions or principles.

It is well known that a great marriage can prevail only with the constancy and determination of a couple's commitment. No less can be said of a great friendship which requires unwearying efforts on each one's part to love and to understand the other. Even Dewey, who insisted that all conclusions should be tentative, unconsciously assented to the intrinsic value of open-mindedness and love when he preached steadfastly in behalf of democracy. It is unfortunate that he contradicted himself by insisting that all values and truths must continuously change. We find the same inconsistency in all his disciples. For example, Neff tells us that it is "a unique purpose of education . . . to keep all avenues to truth open, free, and accessible, as well as to point up the *irreconcilable* conflict between democracy and all forms of absolutism."[18] Here, Neff is unconsciously absolutizing democracy, just as he absolutely rejects any nondemocratic approach to government. Only an absolutist uses such final terms as "irreconcilable" to describe his own philosophical position in contrast with that of others. Although he preaches against certainty, Neff scarcely ever hesitates to show it in his own position.

From the standpoint of autonomy, any individual has a right to believe anything permanently, and without conclusive evidence to prove he is right, as long as he does not use his belief to deny other persons their rights or to hurt them need-lessly. For example, I have a right to affirm permanently the existence of God, to love him, and to believe that he loves me. I would not for one moment pretend that I could prove God's existence to a person who does not want to believe in him. On the grounds of his own claim to openness, would the prag-matist deny me this right? If so, he would be a consummate hypocrite undeserving of his claim to open-mindedness. It is indeed curious that so many pragmatists object to religious faith while at the same time they insist that no one can ever have definite knowledge of anything at all.

I honor any person's right to believe or disbelieve, to tend to his own philosophy and faith. Also, he may criticize my ideas severely as long as he grants me the same privilege and refrains from attempting to change me by any form of coercion or aggression. This is a principle of mutual respect which I be-lieve we must hold to *per fas et nefas*. If anyone is denied this respect while showing it to others, then it is what he deserves if he acquiesces in it.

From whatever angle the pragmatist approaches the individ-ual, he places stifling limitations on his autonomy. No person can build and sustain his identity and sanity if he abuses his intuitive knowledge and private experience. No one can build and expand his autonomy without confidence in his capacity to know. To grow in self-value and autonomy, one must honor his capacity for knowing through his intuitive, private rela-tions with reality. The dogma that a human being can know only that which he can publicly demonstrate is a violation of common sense. This pragmatic tenet is devoid of any founda-tion in factuality or in logic. If it were true, it would mean that I could see and know nothing except that which others agree I have seen and known. I could never learn or come to know anything when I was alone. When not in the presence of others, I could have no cognitive experiences of objective reality. To readers not familiar with pragmatic doctrine, it might seem incredible that any philosopher could actually be this naïve.

Nevertheless, Mr. Neff tells us that "what is true is a matter of scientific formulation, subject to public and critical—as distinguished from private and careless—acceptance."[19]

My wife and I often have delightful, private conversations together. Because of the special beauty and truth in our intimate love, we would not think of displaying it publicly, or of submitting it to any "critical scientific formulation." Is the pragmatist *in practice* so ignorant that he would really disavow all possibility of genuine knowledge of values or truth in his own private experiences? The fact is that we more often plumb to the depths of truth and beauty in private than we do in public. Only a philistine could seriously regard the truths of love as something reducible to a "scientific formulation."

Even so, Neff insists that we can only "believe" what happens to us in private experience; we can never really "know." He says: "The authenticity of what a person may purport to *believe* is scarcely either confirmable or refutable; but what he claims to *know* must, in the pragmatic sense, be capable of demonstration to all who would question, that is, to any impartial, qualified observer."[20]

In other words, I can never really *know* that I love my wife because to really know it, I would first have to be an impartial observer. This is clearly impossible as long as I love her. For certainly, love can never be a passionless, scientific state of personal indifference. On the contrary, love by its very nature will always be a highly partial act. What is more, no impartial observer could possibly recognize love and testify to its reality. This is true for the simple reason that only a lover can recognize love. Certainly, the lover as such is not a scientist but is partial through his very act of affirmation of the value of love. For the loveless observer, the recognition of love is impossible.

Wherever it turns, pragmatism steers perilously close to solipsism. Of course, no pragmatist will ever admit that he regards his own mental impressions as the only existing reality. Indeed, he will expressly object to anyone's equating him with the solipsist. Yet it seems to me that there is no clear distinction between solipsism and the doctrine that nothing can be real or true except what one knows. This would especially seem to be the case in light of the pragmatic dogma that all truth is man-made. Stepping through the mud of relativism, I find not a single truth which does not slip through my fingers and dissolve in the ooze. Neff tells us that we cannot really know anything since there can be absolutely no certainty. Pragmatism, he says, "being primarily a method of knowing, . . . obviously does not begin with any eternal or universal 'truths.' "[21] Nor, of course, can it ever come across any such truths, or end up with them, since universal truths are impossible. We must not forget that truth is only what men "forge," "formulate," or "construct." Moreover, there can be no truths that all men know or ought to know, simply because everything is changing. Hence, no truth can endure.

Neff insists that "what is true is restricted to what is knowable," and that "whatever is at any given time unknowable cannot at the same time be considered true."[22] There seems to be no little incongruity here, considering his immediately preceding insistence that nothing is real or knowable except that which men invent or construct. Lest we become confused in Neff's melee of contradictions, let us bear in mind that pragmatism allows no distinction between reality and human knowledge of reality. A realist insists that many realities in the universe are not contingent upon a human being's knowledge of them. For example, there were galaxies in existence long before a human being invented a telescope powerful enough to observe remote planets and stars. It is true that what has happened in the past has really happened, regardless of our knowledge or ignorance of it. It is inconceivable that past events are dependent upon our "forging" or "constructing" them into reality. Moreover, what is now happening in the world is really happening regardless of how little or how much we may know about it. Of course, the pragmatists reject all of this as simply meaningless speculation, for they will never grant that anything is happening in the universe independently of their thought. Considering this, one wonders why they react so heatedly at being accused of solipsism.

After arguing his premise that certain knowledge is impossible, the pragmatist proceeds to ignore it in virtually everything else he says. For example, he tells us:

Truth means scientific success, or as we ordinarily say, "verification," with all that this term implies. It is what emerges from the critical employment of the best methods that we can develop. It is a social product, not in the sense that a majority happens to accept a given belief, but in the sense that no belief can be called true unless it is capable of compelling the *universal* assent of those who understand.[23]

Here, he eradicates the last vestige of meaning in the individual's private knowledge of himself and the world. No one can possibly know anything until he has compelled the "universal assent of those who understand." No one can have any knowledge of reality unless everyone else has it, unless everyone "capable of understanding" also knows what he knows. For all knowledge, the pragmatist asserts, is a "social product," or else it is nothing at all, or merely illusion. Attempting to defend this dogma, Neff tells us that "to speak of an 'unverifiable truth' would be to exhibit an ill-becoming precociousness or to engage in a contradiction of terms, if not to talk nonsense."[24]

If I may exhibit my own "precociousness," how would Neff go about verifying anything at all? How is verification possible if, in this world of "omnipresent change," there is no evidence that can endure? How can science repeat its experiments if everything constantly changes? How is it possible for a scientist to work under identical circumstances with the same materials, or with the same causes and effects? If no realities can abide, how can any evidences be repeated? How can anyone act on the basis of constant change? Since there can be no definite knowledge of definite, enduring facts, how can a person possibly be an expert in anything? The pragmatists categorically reject a priori truths and self-evident facts. Rejecting essences and abiding realities, they insist that no proposition is intrinsically true or false. They tell us that nothing exists which is true in and of itself; nor is there anything which is valuable in and of itself. It is naïve, they tell us, to speak of "facts which speak for themselves." On the contrary, an idea is true only if and when it "works." The truth of an idea is measured only by its consequences when it is applied in action. If its consequences in action bring a "satisfactory" solution to a problem, the idea is true.

This is all very well, except, is it not a well-known fact that persons with adequate power can make many false and immoral ideas work, simply by forcing situations? For example, Hitler was criticized for using inefficient tactics in his efforts to extinguish the Jews. If he had been more efficient, he could have "solved the Jewish problem" to the satisfaction of himself and the majority of Germans. In other words, his heinous project would have succeeded if he had been more insightful into how to get things done. I am reminded of the thief who went through life stealing the savings of persons who had earned their income honestly by the sweat of their brows. Besides being an artist at robbing money, this crook also mastered the technique of never getting caught. When he found himself running low on funds, he "solved" this problem, to his own "satisfaction," simply by taking from others money that did not belong to him by any moral standard of possession. Then, he would satisfy himself by squandering it on wine, women, and song. This crook was never caught—we learn only from his memoirs how much satisfaction his ideas brought him and how pleasantly he made them "work."

Dewey was fond of using the term "satisfaction" as the criterion for judging the consequences of an idea applied in action. However, he is notorious for having ignored the ambiguity of this term. Are there not as many satisfied criminals as there are satisfied saints?

I do not doubt that morally true ideas will work if they are applied in practice by intelligent and sincere persons. However, we are grossly naïve if we close our eyes to the fact that immoral ideas can be made to work politically and financially by ruthless men of power. This is especially true when ruthless men enjoy the condonance and cooperation of masses of weaklings and cowards.

If there are no intrinsic truths or values, how can the consequences of one idea in practice be *intrinsically* any better or worse than the consequences of any other? Pragmatists succeed in tricking nobody by transferring values from essences to consequences. For if there are no moral essences, then the consequences of one act are never *essentially* any more moral or less moral than those of the opposite act. And where would this leave us? We would necessarily have to conclude that there are no distinguishable values at all.

A self-evident truth is one grounded in pure reason or fact, which is in no need of demonstration or proof. In other words, it is a truth which simply *is* a truth in and of itself. People with adequate intuition can apprehend it merely by using the mysterious powers of the mind. Pragmatism, however, rejects the mind, berates intuition, and prides itself on vetoing all things mystical or magical. Since no one can explain intuition, and since it cannot be demonstrated to those who do not have it, we must reject it altogether as unscientific.

At this point, the realist's hope of ever communicating with the pragmatist sinks. For clearly, it is an egregious intellectual modesty that would deny a human being the right to know something short of perfect understanding or proof. No person needs to explain love before he can know what love is. It is not necessary to explain a sunset in order to know that a sunset *is*. No one needs to explain an apple in order to know that apples are apples. It is ridiculous to deny the individual's capacity for intuitive awareness of himself and the world. The assumption that one must reject knowledge that he cannot communicate to others is a criminal attack upon the very premise of individual integrity and selfhood as an ideal. A human being who is innocent of a crime falsely charged against him must honor his innocence whether or not he can prove it publicly. If it is impossible for him scientifically and socially to demonstrate his innocence, he should stand by himself steadfastly in his private knowledge of the truth that the charges are false. By the same logic, he should recognize his guilt when he is guilty, even if society regards him as innocent. In its assumption that nothing is true except that which can be publicly attested, Dewey's social psychology is simply barbarian.

Pragmatists first tell us that there are no intrinsic truths or values. Then, they tell us that intuitive knowledge is never reliable because it is strictly subjective and relative. Then further, they tell us that there can never be any certain knowledge of reality or truth. And finally, they tell us that "truth is social." Adding these contradictions together, they tell us that knowledge is legitimate only when it "is capable of compelling the universal assent of those who understand."

The apex of absurdity has almost been reached. From this giddy height of unreason, let me pause and try to clear my mind.

If there are no facts that speak for themselves, how is verification possible? If nothing is a fact or a truth in and of itself, what is true at all? If no propositions are inherently true, the principles of verification themselves are neither this nor that, and where does this leave us? What can Dewey possibly mean when he speaks of "the universal assent of those who understand"? Understand what? How can there be any understanding without knowledge? How can we know one thing from another if nothing is definitely and intrinsically different from anything else? If definite or certain knowledge is impossible, what is there to "compel" this "universal assent"? Furthermore, if there are no universal truths, how can or why should there be any universal assent?

The pragmatist tells us that his doctrine is not a philosophy of "reality," that we are mistaken if we take it as such. On the contrary, says Neff, any notions of reality *as such* "are found to be superfluous except as they are recognized as poetic adornments. . . . In so far as pragmatism is basically a *method or procedure* for determining the meaning of an idea, as distinguished from being a body of fixed doctrines or dogmas, most pragmatists are wary of committing themselves to any sort of metaphysics."[25] Neff is simply rephrasing the assertion of Dewey that "the chief characteristic trait of the pragmatic notion of reality is precisely that no theory of Reality in general . . . is possible or needed."[26]

In brief, the pragmatist would like us to believe that he has no concern for understanding the basic characteristics of reality as such. Rather, he would have us consider his doctrine

entirely as a philosophy of "process of knowledge," "procedures of inquiry," "problem solving techniques," and "methods
of testing."

I think hardly anyone who looks closely at the body of
pragmatic dogmas which parade under the euphemistic term
"assumptions" will be convinced of this. When the pragmatist
says, *"All* reality is experience," what is he talking about if not
about reality as such? When he says, *"All* reality is a continuum," how can he claim that he is not making a judgment
about reality? When he says, "The essence of reality is change,"
what is he if not a metaphysician? There is an outright intellectual hypocrisy in the unwillingness of the pragmatist to
stand honestly behind his own fundamental philosophical asser-
tions. In the first place, any act of philosophizing takes place
within nature and is itself a part of reality. From this it would
follow that the pragmatic claim to intellectual purity or detachment is a myth. In the second place, no one can think
about anything at all (pragmatically or otherwise) without in
some sense thinking about reality. If the pragmatist's claim—
that he is never talking about reality as such—is true, then
just what is he talking about? Dewey's statement that *no theory
of reality in general is possible or needed* is itself a very definite
and radical statement about the nature of reality. It clearly
implies that it is impossible for us to have any definite knowledge of the basic aspects of reality, which is theoretically
nihilistic. This is tantamount to saying that, in reality, there is
no knowable reality at all. Dewey is also implying that there
would be no need for such knowledge even if it were possible.
Following this line of reasoning, we end up in a conceptual
position of negation, denying both the possibility of real
knowledge and the worthwhileness of having it. This pragmatic
claim of making no definite claims is a counterfeit position,
which is not exactly lacking in guile. Actually, the pragmatist
is not as solely preoccupied with matters of methods and procedures as he would like us to believe. What is more, such a
preoccupation with mere methodology and procedures would
be impractical and inhuman. What a waste of time, to devote

all of one's life only to studying process, without any concern for the knowledge of reality to be gained through that process!

There can be no ground for autonomy in a mere study of methods. Throughout his lifetime, a human being must have objectives to accomplish, to expand and enrich his self-meaning and self-value. His personal objectives must be the *ends* of his methods and procedures. No person can fulfill himself while attending only to means. Indeed, the very term "means" is unintelligible except insofar as it is related to the accomplishment of some end. I have already indicated that autonomy requires the pursuit of new knowledge. It is an unquestionable fact, however, that the will to live cannot thrive on pursuit alone. Some ends have to be accomplished successfully, all along. It is true that some frustration and tension are essential to keeping one in the state of mind to seek and to strive. A wholly satisfied or fulfilled person would have no motive or need to strive. In a state of total satisfaction, one would become static; one would vegetate or cease to grow. A mastery of the methods and procedures of acquiring knowledge is essential to a growing autonomy. But what is more important is the end purpose of employing methods in the first place, namely, the progressive acquisition of true knowledge of reality, which gives one the power to fulfill his essential needs and desires in life. In this respect, pragmatism is entirely too negative and narrow a philosophy for the person who would be autonomous.

Genuine autonomy can be built only on a solid foundation of objective truth. The least requirement would be an acknowledgment of the fact that an objective knowledge of reality is possible. In fact, autonomy depends directly upon a knowledge of the most essential moral and psychological truths. It also depends upon the individual's accomplishment of his essential ends. This means not only the progressive acquisition of new meanings, values, and beauties in the endeavor of life, but also the *conservation* of these things in an ever-expanding identity of oneself in the world. Real personal growth builds onto an *enduring* foundation of essential knowledge and love.

5.

Moral Truth: A Fickle Mistress

I BEGAN the writing of this book with the presupposition that true moral knowledge is possible. If philosophy of morality could rest on no objective facts, laws, and principles, then it would be ridiculous that we should even discuss the matter, for the simple reason that there could be no falsehoods and truths to discuss. If all moral judgments were merely arbitrary, then any concept of autonomy also would be merely arbitrary; hence, no person could be factually or logically any more or less autonomous than any other. A viable concept of autonomy requires truth. If morality were reducible to simply a question of differences in taste, any one morality would be as true as any other; consequently, there could be no moral truth whatever. There could be no truth because there could be no falsehood, and therefore no meaningful distinctions for making comparative judgments. If relativism were true, all moral standards would be merely arbitrary just as we find them to be in Sartre, Dewey, and Russell. In this work, I am concerned with the establishment of a universally valid standard.

It is curious that Sartre, Dewey, and Russell have written at such great lengths on mankind's moral problems. It would seem that these men should be conscious that such an endeavor is a waste of time, if the premises of their own nihilism were fundamentally the truth. Three years ago, Sartre and Russell conducted an internationally noted mock trial in Stockholm, Sweden. With a stacked jury and preestablished verdict, they found President Johnson of the United States to be a "war criminal" guilty of wanton "cruelty" and "aggression" against the innocent (?) Communists in South Vietnam. To me this exemplifies the type of moral judgment that is in essence truly arbitrary. If there are no moral standards that are objectively valid, such as these nihilists insist is the case, then on what *grounds* can they object to anyone's behavior as "aggressive," "criminal," or "cruel"? Such recriminatory judgments automatically presuppose that there are objective distinctions between moral and immoral motives and acts. To insist on one hand that moral truth reduces to mere subjective tastes, but then on the other to condemn one's adversaries for objective immorality—this, indeed, establishes beyond a doubt the fact that there *are* arbitrary judgments in the minds of even the prize-winning philosophers. Both Sartre and Russell have won the Nobel Prize for their literature on many topics, not the least of which is their high-sounding moralizing, which sometimes appears like a desire to propagate or improve upon the Sermon on the Mount. Yet, both categorically reject any rational basis for moral law, for both insist that any standard whatever is merely arbitrary and spurious. Were their fundamental premises true, any distinction between right and wrong would be purely specious and whimsical. The only universal standard would be the standard that there can be no objective standard, that all moral argument is a mere quibble of conflicting tastes.

Both of these esteemed philosophers take entirely for granted that they have objective reasons for renouncing objectivity in morals; or to put it differently, they write as though they have a sound standard by which to undermine all moral standards. I myself cannot imagine how their theory of relativity can have any moorings in reality since it itself is based upon no standard that is objectively valid, i.e., grounded in factuality and logic. Of course, there is *one* concept of relativity that makes sense, namely, the assumption that a person's moral knowledge must be relative to his experience. As stated earlier, every individual's knowledge is relative to three things: (1) his inherent capacity to learn, (2) his opportunity to learn, and (3) his willingness or unwillingness to learn. There can be no reasonable doubt that people vary greatly in their moral beliefs and knowledge, simply because their experience varies greatly with regard to these three factors. We would be simpletons or tyrants if we demanded that people behave in ways that are totally unknown to them. Certainly, we could not reasonably hold responsible for behaving in better ways anyone who has had no opportunity to learn that there are better ways to behave. However, the fact that we may be ignorant of moral ideals does not mean that such ideals are unreal, as the nihilists claim. From the positions of Dewey, Sartre, and Russell, we can conclude only that there are no objectively valid ideals whatever, for from their standpoint, there is no meaningful distinction between what the individual *desires* to do and what he *ought* to do.

Russell tells us that *"the good life is one inspired by love and guided by knowledge."*[1] This strikes me as a perfectly sensible thing to say. However, it is an unfortunate remark for Russell to make since he precedes it with a thoroughgoing renunciation of any possibility of genuine knowledge about the nature of love and goodness. For example, in his *Philosophy,* he tells us that "men desire all sorts of things, and in themselves all desires, taken singly, are on a level (i.e., the *same* level)."[2] Therefore, we must realize that "there is no *reason* to prefer the satisfaction of one to the satisfaction of another."[3]

Russell is siding with Sartre and Dewey to say that there are no intrinsic values. This means that no motive, desire, or action is intrinsically any better or worse than any other. For example, a vicious, insane desire to kill one's neighbor is not intrinsically any worse than a kindly disposition to help him.

Russell's whole philosophy is oriented around a rigid scientism. Like the pragmatists, he too believes that there is no legitimate knowledge outside the boundaries of science. However, while the pragmatists equate moral right with scientific insight, Russell insists that all moral and artistic perceptions are entirely subjective and, therefore, are completely outside the realm of scientific understanding. Dewey regards moral insights as reducible to a science; Russell insists that there can be no moral insights at all. For Dewey, a desire is moral if it produces public "satisfaction." Or more exactly, a desire is moral if it brings satisfaction to pragmatic scientists. This means that the desirability of the desire can be demonstrated rigorously. However, Russell finds nothing in human desires and motives that is not totally personal and temperamental. According to him, tastes and desires can in no way be objectively compared and evaluated. Therefore, he tells us that "ethics is traditionally a department of philosophy, and that is my reason for discussing it. I hardly think myself," however, "that it ought to be included in the domain of philosophy. . . ."[4] In other words, moral knowledge is simply impossible.

Like Dewey, Russell rejects intuition as a legitimate way of knowing. Science, and science only, can provide us with genuine knowledge of reality. Regarding morality, he insists that

science has nothing to say about values. . . .Science can tell us much about the *means* of realizing our desires, but it cannot say that one desire is preferable to another. . . .when we assert that this or that has "value," we are giving expression to our own emotions, not to a fact which would still be true if our personal feelings were different. . . .

When a man says "this is good in itself," he *seems* to be making a statement, just as much as if he said "this is square" or "this is sweet." I believe this to be a mistake. I think that what the man really means is: "I wish everybody to desire this," or rather "Would that everybody desired this." If what he says is interpreted as a statement, it is merely an affirmation of his own personal wish; if, on the other hand, it is interpreted in a general way [i.e., as a judgment of moral truth], it states nothing, but merely desires something. The wish . . . is personal, but what it desires is universal. It is, I think, this curious interlocking of the particular and the universal which has caused so much confusion in ethics. . . .

The consequences of this doctrine are considerable. In the first place, there can be no such thing as "sin" . . . ; what one man calls "sin" another may call "virtue," and though they may dislike each other on account of this difference, neither can convict the other of intellectual error.[5]

From the above, we may summarize Russell's theoretical position on morals in four simple propositions. They are: (1) No desire is intrinsically preferable to any other (that is, there is no difference between the desired and the desirable); (2) there is no sin; (3) there is no virtue; and (4) there is no right or wrong.

One of the demands of a realistic philosophy of ethics is that we make our practical conduct in daily life jibe with our academic theories. There can be no doubt that Russell does not honor this nihilistic, antimoral philosophy in his own daily life. In theory, he tells us that ethics has nothing to say about moral truth, since the whole idea of ethics is only a semantical illusion. On the contrary, he says, ethics reduces only to the art of persuasion or exhortation; it is successful when one entices another to share or approve of his own personal tastes and desires. But beyond this, ethics is only a useless disputation of impulses and wishes.

Russell's moral pronouncements do not agree with this theory, even occasionally. Today there are few men in the world more widely known for their angry moral commentaries and preachings. Russell and Sartre stand alike, as two radical nihilists, undermining the possibility of morality while at the same time passionately attacking this and that unjust cause.

Equally as inconsistent, pragmatist Dewey never held to his own theory that moral insights are accessible only to scientists. Indeed the contrary—he held normal human beings around him responsible for their actions, even those who knew nothing about scientific methods.

Nor do Russell and Sartre hold in practice to their doctrine that ideals are the same as desires. To equate the morally desirable with what men desire is to erase any distinction between what men *do* desire versus what they *ought* to desire (at least, once they are given the opportunity to learn more desirable ways of behaving). Moreover, both Sartre and Russell theoretically deny that there is any intrinsic difference between remaining morally ignorant and becoming wise. This is to say, there are no ideal truths or values which *all* of us ought to have a chance to come to know and to live by. In short, there can be no moral progress, for any given way of life is just as moral (or immoral) as any other way of life.

In his *Anti-Semite and Jew,* Sartre condemns as immoral and unreasonable all people who discriminate against and harass the Jews. Also, he attacks as "inauthentic" the character of the Jewish individual who surrenders cowardly to his enemy's efforts to degrade him. For one, I entirely concur with this judgment. I regard it as the moral duty of every person to treat all others with a reasonable respect for their essential needs. However, I wonder on what grounds Sartre can object to the mistreatment of the Jews, considering his theoretical position that there are no essential moral values. From the standpoint of his theory, there can be no such thing as immoral treatment of anyone. Indeed, how can there be if all judgments of right and wrong are strictly relative and arbitrary? Sartre in effect slaps his own face. He theoretically condones as justifiable the very actions which in practice he passionately attacks as pernicious and destructive. If his theory were correct, then no way of treating a Jew (or anyone else) could be any more justifiable, or less justifiable, on objective grounds, than any other treatment.

In practice, Russell, Sartre, and Dewey have ignored their own theories; or at least they have judged others by different criteria than they have judged themselves. There can be no genuine autonomy built on such arbitrary moral habits—it is a false autonomy that does not judge itself as it judges others. The nihilists allow only themselves the prerogative of amoral and arbitrary living. They have stinging recriminations and criticisms ready for all who, in their judgment, act in "immoral" and "unreasonable" ways. In theory, Russell clearly says that there is no "reason" to behave one way rather than another.[6] I find the incongruities in his life nothing less than embarrassing.

Dewey lived by the assumption that people in general can and should respect moral principles and values which they can learn intuitively, granted that they have any chance at all and that they *choose* to learn. Sartre and Russell also turn unconsciously to this *via media* of moral education, i.e., that it is possible for persons to acquire objectively valid moral knowledge, and that people in general can acquire it through intuition when they have adequate opportunities to learn. Although he may deny this in theory, no human being can consistently deny it in practice without losing his sanity.

Nevertheless, let Russell speak for himself in defense of his nihilism. In *Philosophy*, he asks us to realize that

the rules of morals differ according to the age, the race, and the creed of the community concerned. . . .Even within a homogeneous community differences of opinion arise. Should a man kill his wife's lover? The Church says no, the law says no, and common sense says no; yet many people would say yes, and juries often refuse to condemn. These doubtful cases arise when a moral rule is in process of changing.

No realist would deny this. Every educated person knows that legal "rules" change from time to time and place to place. However, is Russell asking us to deduce from *this* the conclusion that *there is no moral truth* about whether the man should, or should not, kill his wife's lover?

He goes on: ". . . in a given community, an ethic which does not lead to the moral rules accepted by that community is considered immoral. It does not, of course, follow that such an ethic is in fact false, since the moral rules of that community may be undesirable."

It is pleasant to hear Russell admit that some ways of behaving are intrinsically undesirable. Precisely what, however, is he now doing with logic? Is he consciously allowing, after all, that some ways of behaving are *intrinsically* undesirable (evil), and that there is a moral difference between the ideally desirable and the actually desired? If so, is he not switching his ground, as all nihilists regularly do? He seems to allow that there is a moral *truth,* that a community's or individual's ethic can be "false."

He continues: "Some tribes of head-hunters hold that no man should marry until he can bring to the wedding the head of an enemy slain by himself. Those who question this moral rule are held to be encouraging licence and lowering the standard of manliness. Nevertheless, we should not demand of an ethic that it should justify the moral rules of head-hunters."

I should hope not! The question is, however: Is Russell really objecting to headhunting, and if so, is it on some grounds other than his merely subjective taste? *Should* we object? He implies that we should "demand" certain things of an ethic. What should we demand? What can and should we demand of an ethic without being merely arbitrary and subjective?

He goes on: "Perhaps the best way to approach the subject of ethics is to ask what is meant when a person says: 'You *ought* to do so-and-so' or 'I *ought* to do so-and-so'."

This makes extremely good sense. However, I am wondering what Russell means when he uses the term "ought." When he finishes with it, will it have any moral meaning left? He continues: "Primarily, a sentence of this sort has an emotional content; it means 'this is the act towards which I feel the emotion of approval'. But we do not wish to leave the matter there; we want to find something more objective and systematic and constant than a personal emotion."

But what *is* this "something more objective"? He has said that all desires "are on the same level," that "there is no reason to prefer the satisfaction of one to the satisfaction of another." If this is the case, then what is it that can be more "objective and systematic and constant than a personal emotion"?

It is, Russell answers, the fact that "when we consider not a single desire but a group of desires, there is this difference, that sometimes all the desires in a group can be satisfied, whereas in other cases the satisfaction of some of the desires in the group is incompatible with that of others."

Here, Russell is referring to moral "good" as those "things *desired* by the whole of a social group." I do not know how he could possibly mean it to be taken otherwise, for he finishes: "It is evident, therefore, that there can be more good in a world where the desires of different individuals harmonise than in one where they conflict. The supreme moral rule should, therefore, be: *Act so as to produce harmonious rather than discordant desires.*"[7]

I have no objections to harmony in human relations, provided it is not achieved by squelching the creativity and freedom of righteous individuals. However, I believe Mr. Russell's principle is ambiguous at best, and may be used to justify the most hideous crimes at worst (though of course he would not intend it to be so used). After first asserting that custom does not necessarily make right, he then tells us that the only moral motive which all of us should have is adjustment to social harmony. Imagine the Lord Jesus fulfilling his mission by always producing "harmonious rather than discordant desires." Had Socrates abided by Russell's principle, he would never have drunk the hemlock—simply because he would never have countered any social traditions in the first place. If Russell were caught by the headhunters, would he "harmonise" with their custom, so as not to produce "discordant desires"? If not, why not? After all, he himself tells us that morality is nothing except emotions. The cannibals' desire to eat him is neither good nor bad—it is simply a matter of taste. Their emotions and tastes, therefore, are neither better nor worse than Russell's. As a matter of fact, his own personal life is itself the refutation of his principle of harmony. Few people in England have produced more social discordancy than Russell himself. He is known for his rebelliousness, not for his conformity. He is known basically for what he attacks, not for what he approves. Indeed, considering his constant shifting and inconsistency, it is often impossible to discern what he definitely believes in and wants.

With this one principle, Russell contradicts his own moral nihilism; for he is saying, in effect: My desire for harmony is what *all* men *ought* to desire; harmony is intrinsically desirable; it is the ideal moral good.

Unfortunately, the search for viable moral principles in Russell is fruitless. Like Dewey, he ends up identifying moral truth with a satisfied society. Next to tyrannical governments and institutions, this is the most dangerous threat in modern life to the individual's autonomy. For certainly, no person can harmonize always with those around him and sustain his identity and integrity. No one can safely peg his life on the democratic principle that one ought always to be guided by majority opinion. In the first place, the assumption that prevailing opinion is always right is false. In fact, there is much historical evidence that it is very often wrong. In the second place, there is no reason to conclude that the individual has a moral obligation to conform to the majority will when it is wrong. In practice, Russell himself knows this and acts accordingly. In fact, he seems to have a penchant for creating antagonism and discordancy with prevailing opinion, wherever he goes.

Here, I must leave Russell and his brand of autonomy for the Fates. In summary, it should be evident that his relativism can never serve as a rational basis for personal integrity. If his theory were true, it would efface all meaningful distinctions between right and wrong. As mentioned earlier, it is obvious that he himself ignores his own theory in practice, for he certainly does not regard his own moral judgments as merely arbitrary and subjective.

Returning to pragmatism, I find a complete denial that autonomy is available to anyone but the scientist. For example, in his "First Principles for a Modern Philosophy of Education," Earl Cunningham insists that "existence can be attributed only to that which is quantitatively measurable."[8] This, of course, would necessarily lead to the conclusion that love, happiness, and dignity cannot possibly exist since such things certainly are never subject to quantitative measurement. Obviously, love is a quality, not a quantity; and it can be apprehended as such only intuitively, or it can never be apprehended at all. Nonetheless, echoing Dewey, Cunningham tells us that "to be genuine and informative," moral knowledge "must be capable of public verification."[9] In other words, moral problems have to do only with the individual's relations to society, never with his own private relations with himself. This would necessarily lead us to conclude that the individual is accountable only to society, never to himself; he must integrate with the group, rather than with himself. This smacks of the socialist assumption that "the dominant need of the individual is to belong socially," or to be accepted by a group.[10]

I regard this as a very dangerous falsehood which is breeding untold numbers of neurotic people in our society. The plain truth is: the dominant need of any individual is personal integrity, without which genuine social belongingness is categorically impossible. The person who stabs a knife in the back of his own conscience in order to be socially accepted and financially secure cannot really belong at all. On the contrary, his belongingness is a myth, a front, based on social roots that are either shallow or totally fraudulent. Unless one first belongs to himself, he can never belong genuinely to any others. There can be no self-fulfillment in outward adjustment while inwardly one is alienated from himself. Any social ethic that requires its members to wear masks and to falsify themselves in order to be accepted is false. Honest autonomy has enough problems of its own without adding the complication of deceiving oneself and others. For one thing, there is the pain of the price one must pay for living with unpopular truth. However, any attempt at autonomy through self-deception and mutilation is doomed to failure; its price, in the end, is much more painful and destructive than that of living by the truth. One should rather die a social failure but intact with himself than live socially "adjusted" but inwardly bereft.

Pragmatist Frederick Neff tells us that moral truth " 'emerges' from the testing of hypotheses, which is to say that it is not antecedent to investigation."[11] I have already referred to pragmatism's doctrine that all truths are man-made. From this viewpoint, no moral ideals can have objective reality or differ intrinsically from personal desires. In a word, the headhunting ideals of the cannibals are intrinsically no better or worse than the cooperative love of more civilized peoples. Neff must consistently ignore this theory in his own daily social relations. He often forgets his nihilistic moral theory and, in practice, proceeds to beat the air of science. For example, he tells us that a moral statement "that purports to be true is one which is convertible into a proposition formulated as a hypothesis, the testing of which will bear out the prediction that the proposition claims to be true."[12] This means, apparently, that when I have a moral problem, I must form as many hypotheses as scientific thinkers can suggest regarding possible ways to solve it. Then, I must rephrase each of these hypothetical solutions in the form of a proposition that can be scientifically tested. True to their usual form, however, the pragmatists seldom go into any discussion about how this method can be applied to solving *concrete* and *real* moral problems.

Let us consider that I am tempted to commit a murder. In this case, as a pragmatist I should form two hypotheses: (1) that I should commit the murder, to achieve my desired ends, and (2) that I should *not* commit the murder, to achieve my desired ends (for there may be more efficacious and less troublesome means). Of course, as a scientist I must test *both* hypotheses, then compare the outcome of each, by evaluating their consequences with regard to a solution of my problem. My only question is, How can I possibly test *both* of these hypotheses? If I commit the murder, certainly there will then be many consequences to study. However, it will then be effectually impossible to test the other hypothesis, i.e., that of never committing the murder. For how can one both commit a murder and not commit it? As a realist, I cannot help insisting that this is equally the case with all serious moral problems. For example, if I am tempted to commit a theft, I cannot both steal the desired object and not steal it. Who can both commit adultery and not commit adultery? If I committed adultery, I could never test precisely how different the consequences would have been from those of never committing the act. Or, suppose that I become wearied of life. Imagine that I am afflicted with great suffering, both physical and mental, and am tempted to commit suicide to escape from my pain. At the same time, I know that I have responsibilities to those around me. Consequently, I wonder if I should strive on with life, despite my pain. Obviously, I cannot both commit suicide and continue to live. No matter which alternative I choose to act on, my first choice negates the possibility of acting on the other. If I were dead, I could not test the alternative consequences of remaining alive; and if I chose to live, I could not test the consequences of taking my life.

At this point I might be accused of oversimplifying the methods of science. However, no pragmatist could justifiably accuse me of such without resorting inevitably to the recognition of intuition as a legitimate means of knowing, plus recognizing that there are intrinsic moral values and truths. After all, it is the pragmatist, not I, who insists on reducing morality to a strictly empirical science. Empirical science demands the testing of *all* relevant hypotheses, which in matters of morality is simply impossible without resort to intuition. If a man cannot *intuit* that committing a murder will needlessly complicate his life (we shall not mention the victim), then certainly *acting* on the murder hypothesis cannot rescue him from trouble.

According to Randall and Buchler, pragmatism says: "A problem is significant or genuine" only "if the possible answers to it are verifiable, that is, if it is capable of scientific investigation."[13] From this one should infer that any problems not solvable by scientific methods are unimportant and unreal. Frederick Neff puts it in these words: "To subject ideas to testing is to reveal whatever are pseudo-problems, which then either evaporate or are quickly resolved."[14]

I frankly am amazed at how casually some pragmatists can dispense with God. The question of whether God exists is infinitely important to those of us who cherish his name. Yet, it certainly is not a question capable of being answered by neutral scientists who would reduce him to a finite object for experimentation. Since God is infinite, he can never be encompassed by any finite mind. He may be at best only partially understood by those who believe in him and experience the joy and power of religious love. Even in its most mature stages, our knowledge of God will always be a mixture of faith, logic, and intellectual adumbration—no person's knowledge of him is complete, and never can be. The autonomous believer will make no pretension to scientifically demonstrating the existence of God. He knows that God cannot be dissected, measured, and classified as though he were merely another laboratory project. God can never be apprehended by the cold neutrality which is proper to the objective scientist. Neff greatly misunderstands the problem of God's existence in calling it a "pseudo-problem." According to him, my need to love God is a pseudo-need.

Dewey tells us that scientific "experimentation enters into determination of every warranted proposition."[15] Also, he says that "if certain [scientific] operations are performed, then certain phenomena having determinate properties will be observed."[16] Or, as Neff says, rewording Dewey: "The extent to which a proposition has meaning . . . lies in the effectiveness of its operation; to say that a proposition is true, i.e., has 'warrantable assertability,' is to say that the results that it predicts actually do occur."[17]

From this it would follow that the question of God's existence cannot be philosophically meaningful, for obviously no scientific experiment can demonstrate whether or not God exists. It is simply impossible to subject him to experimentation; no "operations" can be "performed" with him, least of all by sceptics who do not even care about the reality or worthwhileness of his being. We can in no way manipulate God as laboratory material in order that his "determinate properties will be observed." The proposition that God exists can have no "warrantable assertability" in this pragmatic sense—that it "predicts what actually occurs."

I certainly can predict that new power and meaning will enter into the person who *decides* to have faith in God. There are untold numbers of people who will testify to this fact. No observant person could fail to see the constructive changes that are effected in people's lives through positive faith. However, our faith in God can in no way represent a *manipulation* of him as an experimental object. Rather, it must be the seeking of an interpersonal relationship with him; and certainly, it can be a meaningful experience only for the believing seeker, never for the doubter. Our faith is in the power of God to explain us, not in any power we might have to explain him. Primarily, we believe in his power to conserve the values and meanings which we know can be found only in love for him.

According to Neff, however, all of this is "sheer nonsense," or mere subjective "romanticism" totally lacking in "warrantable assertability." The question of God's existence should be recognized as a "pseudo-problem" that should "either evaporate or be quickly resolved."[18] And by "quickly resolved," he of course means put out of our minds.

The redoubtable William James constituted an exception to

this coldly atheistic disposition of pragmatists in general. Like Dewey, James insisted that "the hypothesis that works is the *true* one."[19] In contrast to Dewey, however, he believed that the hypothesis of a loving God works to bring greater richness and maturity into the lives of intelligent and sincere people. As he himself put it:

The pragmatic method . . . is to try to interpret each notion by tracing its respective practical consequences. What difference would it practically make to any one if this notion rather than that notion were true? If no practical difference whatever can be traced, then the alternatives mean practically the same thing, and all dispute is idle. Whenever a dispute is serious, we ought to be able to show some practical difference that must follow from one side or the other's being right.[20]

There is a great deal of truth and practical wisdom in this statement. As for its application in religion, people who have discovered the uplifting power of love for God *know* that it makes life infinitely more important than it previously seemed to be. Nothing can "work miracles" in the life of the spirit more than a deep and decisive devotion to God. It is unfortunate, in this respect, that James contradicted himself by doing away with intrinsic values. It is obvious that, like Dewey, he regarded "usefulness," "workability," and "practical results" as the criteria for measuring the validity of moral ideas in action. But as it happens, such criteria are meaningless if the results of one action are not *intrinsically* more practical, useful, and workable than the results of other actions. James returns us to where Dewey left us—in a neverland of "values," none of which is essentially different from any other.

Neff tells us that "James evidently meant that if such belief wrought observable changes for good in people's lives, it was accordingly true." He rejects this as a betrayal of true pragmatism and says that "what was being tested was not whether God exists but whether there was a belief that God exists, which belief might then understandably affect conduct."[21] He then tells us that "James had very definite romantic attachments and inclinations which often obscured what pragmatic commitments he claimed, and his interpretation of moral and religious matters scarcely represents the viewpoint of present-day pragmatism."[22]

It is now clear that, from a strictly pragmatic view, there can be no room in autonomy for freedom of the will to *believe*. For the pragmatist, the only autonomous man is the scientific man, the ice-hearted agnostic who forms no "romantic attachments and inclinations." To be truly autonomous, one must assent to nothing except to that "which is capable of compelling the universal assent of those who understand." And of course, those who understand are those who know that nothing can be definitely known. *Enfin,* the autonomous man must be the one who knows nothing for certain, commits himself to nothing for certain, hence unshackles himself of any facts, values, or principles that might definitely bind and limit him.

It apparently never enters Neff's mind that there are people whose moral center rests in religious conviction. That we might have a moral relationship with *God* strikes him as childishly sentimental and foolish. No less ridiculous and fanciful to him is the idea that there might be something in life that is worth permanently conserving. When Neff speaks of change, he seems almost religiously to regard it as a godsend, as though it were a guarantee that he will never be bound definitely by anything. There are certain psychological advantages in pragmatism, if one wishes to thrive on the negative. One of them is the fact that if one decides there are no definite truths, then there is no reason why one should feel accountable to anything or anybody.

In the final study, we find pragmatic moral theory hopelessly bogged down. Consider the following contradictions: (1) Moral truth lies in the most useful idea in action; (2) no idea in action is intrinsically any more useful than any other; (3) something is morally true if it can be publicly proved; (4) there are no definite criteria or any facts by which anything can be really proved; (5) we know something is morally true when it is "capable of demonstration to all who would question, that is, to any impartial, qualified observer";[23] (6) there can be no impartial, qualified observer since every point of view is relative, arbitrary, and fallible.

Dewey tells us that moral truth "cannot emerge when there is positive belief as to what is right and what is wrong, for then there is no occasion for reflection."[24]

If this were true, what point would there be in writing endless pages about moral knowledge *which no one can ever have?* True morality, Dewey tells us, has nothing to do with enduring principles or values that are objective and essential. The autonomous man will have no truck with "positive belief as to what is right and what is wrong." For him, morality must navigate a course whereby it steers clear, hits no rocks or shoals of definiteness, clarity, or essential reality. Morality is a *method,* which is ever changing and ever approaching but never arriving. Dewey says: "The need in morals is for specific *methods* of inquiry and of contrivance: Methods of inquiry to locate difficulties and evils; methods of contrivance to form plans to be used as working hypotheses in dealing with them."[25]

It is scarcely possible to understand what is meant here by the term "evils." In denying intrinsic values, Dewey reduces all desirables to desires, and destroys all rational criteria for distinguishing better ones from worse ones. To him, there is no such thing as moral knowledge. There are only "working hypotheses," none of which ever goes beyond the stage of being merely hypothetical. As far as moral *knowledge* is concerned, Dewey allows us no clear distinction between good and evil; he leaves us adrift. I find his criticisms of the illogical and fuzzy moral thinking of nihilism to describe perfectly the contradictions in his own position. He seems to be objecting to the nihilistic philosophy that right is might. Describing this doctrine, he says: "If [one] liking . . . conflicts with some other liking, the strongest wins. There is no question of false and true, of real and seeming, but only of stronger and weaker. The question of which one *should* be stronger is as meaningless as it would be in a cock-fight."[26]

Actually, Dewey is objecting in practice to a vicious doctrine which his own moral theory unwittingly supports all the way. If there are no intrinsic truths and falsehoods, then the nihilistic hypothesis is as valid as any other. If the fundamental premises of pragmatism were true, then the crying out for distinctions between "false and true, real and seeming" would be totally meaningless.

Although Dewey wrote about the subject of individualism on numerous occasions, I cannot recall his ever using the term "moral autonomy." Today no one in progressive-education circles in America is more often quoted than he, despite the fact that he made individual autonomy theoretically impossible. His relativism demolishes any rational distinctions in reason and morality, and is opposed, in effect, to any structure of personality and character that would rest on *abiding* principles and values. In Dewey's concept of persistent change, the individual must avoid resolute adherence to any principles, either in theory or in practice; otherwise, he inevitably would fall behind the times as a blind victim of passé notions. An evolutionary world in which all truths are strictly relative and changing can support no principle whose truth is permanent. Therefore, the quest for autonomy in permanent values and knowledge can result only in emotional and intellectual putrefaction. The world is categorically evolutionary. It is impossible that anything is eternal. Therefore, the only enduring principle is that all principles must be subject to revision. For Dewey, the autonomous man is the totally open man, the antidogmatist, the critical relativist. Such a man is prepared to shift his position at any time, whenever adjustment to his environment calls for it. However, we must bear in mind that Dewey rejects any distinction between the environment and the individual, if by individual we mean a discontinuous and distinct agent. Thus, to be autonomous the individual must reject the traditional notion of autonomy, that he can be a truly distinct agent with an *abiding* identity of his own.

I previously stated that it is impossible for anybody to take this position seriously in practical life. No one can be conscious of himself without logically and existentially separating himself from other persons and things in the world. Moreover, Dewey does not hold consistently to his positon even in theory. Embarrassed by charges that he is nihilistic and irrational, he once again contradicts himself by switching his position back and forth. He tells us:

Morals must be a *growing science* if it is to be a science at all, not merely because all truth has not yet been appropriated by the mind of man, but because *life is a moving affair in which old moral truth ceases to apply.* . . .But the experimental character of moral judgments does not mean *complete* uncertainty and fluidity. *Principles exist as hypotheses with which to experiment.* . . .There is a long record of past experimentation in conduct, and there are cumulative verifications which give many principles a well earned prestige. Lightly to disregard them is the height of foolishness. But social situations alter; and it is also foolish not to observe how old principles actually work under new conditions, and not to modify them so that they will be more effectual instruments in judging new cases.[27]

Here, Dewey swerves close to realism. He *almost* admits that definite moral knowledge is possible. We are told that knowledge of the truth can be "appropriated" by the mind of man (as in contrast to his general position that it is all invented). He tells us that "the experimental character of moral judgments does not mean *complete* uncertainty and fluidity." But then he immediately rebukes the notion that some moral principles might always be followed because they are always true. Although he claims to refute charges of nihilism, he in fact fails to escape from "complete uncertainty and fluidity." To admit to definite knowledge, he would have to admit that some moral principles are inherently true, that is, they are not merely experimental in character and do not change with the flux of customs, fads, and whims. What is more, no one can say that there is not complete uncertainty without admitting that there is some degree of certainty.

Pragmatism cannot divorce itself from moral issues without becoming isolationist and useless. This is indeed much emphasized by the pragmatists themselves. Howbeit, the fact remains that any sensible contribution they might otherwise make to moral dialogue is lost in their nihilism, for neither the social group nor its individual members can think and act responsibly on the basis of flagrant contradictions. Autonomy consists in a basic *inner order,* in an abiding intellectual and emotional *unity,* without which one can neither think nor act coherently enough to realize progressively his essential needs. One need not be a pragmatist in order to be open-minded and critical of old mores and fads. In fact, one must reject pragmatism in order to affirm resolutely the intrinsic truth-value of open-mindedness as a way of life that is definitely better than closed-minded narrowness. Pragmatism cannot support the open-mindedness principle which is its proudest claim. In fact, it cannot definitely support any principle whatever, not even its own negative absolutes, which are logically suicidal. No one can find real moral value in the dogma that there are no certain values. On strictly relativist grounds, there can be no rational objection to a thoroughly lawless and chaotic community of criminals.

Examples of pragmatism's schizophrenia are found in all its representatives who plead for moral wisdom. On the contemporary scene, Charles Frankel enjoys the forefront as a pragmatic moralist, through such prominent books as *The Case for Modern Man* and *The Love of Anxiety.* Like those who preceded him, he denies the possibility of morality on the one hand, but on the other makes eloquent pleas for the good and responsible life. He tells us that

every inquiry, whether in history or the natural sciences, must proceed by taking something for granted. But this does not mean that in every inquiry we take the same assumption for granted. What we leave unquestioned in one context we can very well question in another. The fact that we must make assumptions proves only one thing—that *none* of our knowledge is certain. But while we can *never* attain absolute certainty, we can progressively *correct* the assumptions we make.[28]

Is it not a bit ridiculous to be told that we can know nothing for certain by the same man who in the same paragraph tells us that it is a fact that all men must make assumptions, that all inquiries must proceed on presuppositions, etc., etc.? How can Mr. Frankel know these general truths as facts if no human being can know anything for certain? He tells us: "The fact that we must make assumptions proves only one thing—that *none* of our knowledge is certain." I believe that this is a far from rational inference. The fact that we must make assumptions proves only one thing to me, namely, the *fact* that we must make assumptions, and this is a certain and extremely important fact for everyone to know.

How can we "progressively *correct*" the assumptions we make if we can acquire no definite knowledge of reality with which to make valid corrections?

Frankel elaborately rejects definite knowledge. There can be no facts that really *are* facts, i.e., which are the truth for all men, whether they know it or not. Yet, like his philosophical cohorts (Dewey and Hook), he fills his own books with "facts" and "principles" galore, whose universal validity we are never supposed to question. For example: "Why is it said that the sickness of modern society goes back to the fact that it was born sick, and that all the signposts we have been using to measure our progress have *in fact* been measures of the progress of this disease? Why is it felt that something very fundamental has gone wrong?"[29]

One may well agree with the conclusion that something is wrong in humanity's history. But how is it possible for him to know this, to make this sweeping generalization about history and to declare it to be a fact? How is it possible for one to say such things and really be a pragmatist? First, he insists that no one can safely generalize about history, that we can have no certain knowledge of reality even in the limited sphere of our local community now. Then, he jumps into a realist's shoes and tells us that "something very fundamental has gone wrong" with the human race in all its epochs and places. On what grounds can he make such a judgment and be true to his dogmatic principle that no definite moral knowledge is possible? To say that something very fundamental has gone wrong in human history is to say that there always has been a right way in which it could and should have gone. In other words, true moral ideals have an objective validity transcending history. Through experience, we can come to have a knowledge of these ideals and use them to judge the direction we have taken. This is to say, definite moral knowledge is really possible; it can be cumulative, and we can progressively grow into more enlightened and valuable persons.

In this respect, Frankel's position is hopelessly contradictory. He presupposes what he denies, and denies what he presupposes. On page after page he speaks of things that supposedly no person can ever know; then, he proceeds to show us that he himself knows them and wants us to share his wisdom.

In *Love of Anxiety,* he tells us:

The first characteristic of pragmatism as an attitude toward life . . . is its distrust of doctrines and creeds, its suspicion of words and argumentation. The pragmatist prefers action to talk, he is restless for results, and he normally counts "results" in terms of some physical or visible difference that has been made in the world. . . .Generally speaking, a pragmatist *says nothing about the goals of life.* On the contrary, he seems to suspect that such talk is merely a way of avoiding the real business of life, which is to get down to work. He tends to believe . . . that if the physical side of life is buttoned up neatly, if the safety, convenience, and comfort of life are enhanced, most of the so-called *spiritual* problems will lose their urgency. So he is impatient with people who waste their time and the limited resources of mankind by sitting around asking questions that can never be answered. . . . The pragmatist is suspicious of discussion of the ends of life. . . .he assumes that you are merely whistling in the dark when you talk about all your high purposes but never get down to the question of how to reach them. Indeed, he is convinced that what men accomplish generally depends more on the *methods* they use than on the purposes they profess. . . .It is an open world, a world in which men, if they are strong-willed enough, can will into existence a large part of whatever it is that they desire.

But what is it that the pragmatist thinks that men desire, or *ought* to desire? We come to the ultimate value judgment buried in the pragmatic *Weltanschauung,* the basic reason why *it pays so little attention to questions of ends and purposes.* The great purpose, for the spontaneous pragmatist, is *nothing else but the exercise of human ingenuity and resolution,* nothing else but the solving of problems *whatever they may be. . . .*

If there is any conception of progress, of cumulative improvement, in this glorification of motion, it is the idea of improvement in *Method and Technique,* in knowledge and in power.[30]

I also am suspicious of doctrines and creeds that go unexamined and express themselves aggressively. Too, I place a high value on action and the will to "get down to work." Moreover, I doubt that Frankel has any more concern, as a pragmatist, for results in the practical application of ideas than I have as a realist. Like a typical pragmatist, he talks as though it is only he and his school who are seriously concerned about improving the world and the general life of humanity. I part ways with him when he speaks of "the basic reason [for paying] so little attention to questions of ends and purposes." If he is suspicious of people who talk of high purposes but do not act, then I am equally suspicious of people who act without devoting any critical thought to the spiritual and moral validity of their purposes. I deeply distrust this glorification of "safety, convenience, and comfort," this Philistine philosophy that "if the physical side of life is buttoned up neatly, . . . the so-called *spiritual* problems will lose their urgency."

Why does Frankel disparage the urgency of the spiritual life with his term "so-called"? The tenor of his volumes is unmistakably atheistic and secular. But because he has no interest in God or in an immortal life of love, does this mean that those of us who do have such interests are foolish children? If so, I hope to remain a child all the days of my life.

He tells us: "If there is any conception of progress, of cumulative improvement, . . . it is the idea of improvement in Method and Technique."

I myself would like to see some improvement in humanity's general understanding of the ideal goals toward which all of us should strive. Only a pragmatist would capitalize such words as "Method" and "Technique." I sincerely wish Hitler had devoted less time to improving his methods of extinguishing his adversaries and more time to critically questioning the moral validity of his ends. Frankel tells us that pragmatism generally "says nothing about the goals of life." How crude this is. For if we have learned anything at all worth knowing, is it not that the contemplation of man's reason for being alive is what contributes most to our spiritual dignity and uplift-ment?

In keeping with the pragmatic creed, Frankel relativizes all knowledge. He completely does away with the notion that there are some essential and abiding truths. However, his devotion to moralizing is only further evidence that pragma-tism is schizophrenic, that it can never hope to make true moral judgments on the basis of its own fundamental premises. No nihilist, as nihilist, can claim that any of his judgments are essential or true. Yet, Frankel tells us:

If pragmatism as an everyday attitude is to prevail and to succeed, there *has to be* . . . a reservoir of mutual trust and good will in so-ciety, and some fairly *firm* and *restraining* norms of behavior. . . . The *essential* stability and decency of society, and the existence of a *basic* moral consensus, have been the unspoken premises on which popular pragmatism has rested.[31]

Between his "unspoken premises" (the assertion that there are "essential" moral principles and truths) and his dogmatic belief that no moral truths are essential or knowable, is there not a flagrant inconsistency in his reasoning? Can a rational man tell us that "none of our knowledge is certain," then insist that there are "ultimate principles" which should govern our lives? In his spirit of "distrust" of all "doctrines and creeds," Frankel assails all fixed principles as doctrinaire and naïve. Indeed, in his compliance with the pragmatic dogma of change, he can do nothing else. But then, he tells us that cru-cial moral truths are "matters of *ultimate principle*," for ex-ample, "the integration of Negroes into American life."[32] Pragmatism, he admits, cannot always be taken seriously, for there are times when it simply cannot work. For example:

It does not work when decisions of *principle* are involved that can-not be postponed or finessed. For sometimes decisions of principle can be postponed or finessed; but not always. In the case of racial segregation, for example, the issue at stake is not, in fact, this or that limited reform. It is a matter of *principle*—the recognition of the Negro's equal status with all other citizens and his full member-ship in American society.[33]

On this matter of principle, I absolutely agree. With regard to integrating the races and striving for equal opportunity and rights for everyone, our society as a whole has too long postponed and finessed.

However, I am concerned in this book with a moral philosophy that rises above the pragmatic sickness. There is an essential imbecility in a philosophy that contradicts itself wherever it turns.

Herein, I am striving for a set of definite and precisely worded moral principles which no human being can afford to "postpone or finesse" at any time. There is neither beauty nor truth in a philosophy that cannot be put into practice.

Here ends my critical assault on pragmatism. In the following chapters I shall offer a set of positive principles in lieu of relativism's negative absolutes, which are irrational and useless.

PART TWO

The Ethic
of Autonomy

6.

A Universal Need

I CONTEND that there are six principles essential to a sound ethic of personal autonomy. They are:

1. The principle of freedom and integrity of conscience. This states that *the individual should always do what he thinks is right.*
2. The principle of earnestness. This states that *one should always act to make his life as beautiful, meaningful, and valuable as possible.*
3. The principle of equity. This means that *every individual should be self-reflective, should judge himself as cautiously and critically as possible, and should judge others by the same criteria with which he judges himself under the same circumstances.*
4. The principle of the bilateral nature of rights. According to this, *every individual has the right to creative and independent thinking and acting as long as he honors this same right in all others, and as long as in his differences he does not inflict needless harm or suffering on himself or others.*
5. The principle of ward, according to which *the individual has both the right and the duty to defend himself and others against any form of tyranny or injustice, insofar as he is capable.*
6. The principle of love, which simply states that *the individual should respect and love himself as much as pos-*

sible, and also respect and love God and his neighbors as much as possible.

First, I should mention that these principles are not listed in the order of their importance. In fact, I regard the entire ethic as organic, i.e., no one principle must be regarded as any less important than any other. This ethic is effective and valid as a whole, just as an individual is only as autonomous as he is capable of acting as a unified and whole being. The reasons for this should become apparent as I discuss the logic of the principles both separately and in their connections with one another. A friendly minister once suggested that I am slightly blasphemous in putting the principle of love in sixth place. I recall Jesus' admonition that we should love God with all our mind, heart, and soul. He made this the first commandment, and said, " 'A second is like it, You shall love your neighbor as yourself.' " No diminution of attention to God is intended here. On the contrary, I simply have discovered that a person cannot truly worship and serve God if he ignores or negates any of these other principles in his behavior. For example, the first principle (that one should always do what he thinks is right) is of equal importance, for the very substantial reason that it is impossible to act out a true love for God without integrity of conscience. On the other hand, that one should always do what he thinks is right is dangerous and self-destructive if one acts on this principle alone.

It is probably apparent to the reader that the validity of the first principle will depend upon my definition and conception of guilt, and of moral right and wrong. Thus, it would behoove me to define these terms clearly and then to state my reasons in support of the principle.

However, I first should point out that there are philosophers of ethics who definitely believe that this principle is meaningless. Some assume that it is impossible for a person to do anything *other* than what he thinks is right. For example, William Frankena, in his *Ethics,* states:

a man must in the moment of decision do what he thinks is right. He cannot do otherwise. This does not mean that what he does will be right or even that he will not be worthy of blame or punishment. *He simply has no choice,* for he cannot at that moment see any discrepancy between what is right and what he thinks is right. The life of man, even if he would be moral, is not without its risks.[1]

Frankena appears to contradict himself, even to the point of making morality impossible. For how can he say that the individual "in the moment of decision . . . simply has no choice," but also declare that he might "be worthy of blame or punishment"? Where there is no choice, on what grounds could anyone be justly held to blame? Granted, there are conflicting opinions about the possibility of a person's doing what he at the time knows to be wrong, or at least thinks to be wrong. The fact remains, however, that moral responsibility or guilt is impossible if a human being can never do a wrong and know, or think, at the time that he does it that it is wrong. All the courts of law in the land presuppose this to be the case, that one can do a wrong and be conscious at the time of the act that it is wrong. I certainly must insist on this. For if everybody *always* does what he thinks is right, or if no one ever sees a discrepancy between what he thinks is right and what he is doing, then how is it possible for a person ever to experience a feeling of conscience, self-contradiction, self-division, immorality, or hypocrisy? That a human being can do what he at the time thinks is wrong simply means that perversion is possible. Indeed, it is precisely because perversion or immorality is possible that positive morality itself is possible.

Frankena tells us that "at that moment" a decision is made the individual "simply has no choice." If by this he means that a decisive action is a decisive action, he is uttering a mere tautology with which no one can logically disagree. However, we must bear in mind the fact that all our decisions are made in the present moment. Obviously, we do not make past decisions, for they have already been made; nor do we make future decisions, for future decisions can be made only in the future. The only moral, or immoral, decisions that can be made are those which are made in the present, or else there are no choices at all. By throwing out morality "at the moment," Frankena throws out morality *tout à fait*. If there can be no self-contradiction in the present, there can be no self-contradiction ever. If one can never at any moment do what he thinks is wrong, then moral hypocrisy becomes logically inconceivable, for the obvious reason that inconsistency in the moral agent is ruled out as impossible at *any* given moment in his life.

From my own experience I know that a human being can be perverse. This means that one not only can be inconsistent with his past self but can divide and contradict himself at the present moment. One can hypocritically defy his own conscience, be double-minded, and can weaken his own autonomy through the very act of dividing himself, emotionally and intellectually. On certain past occasions, I have acted hypocritically and was conscious of my hypocrisy at the time. In effect, Frankena is telling us that all persons have pure integrity all the time, since there is never a moment in which anyone can morally divide or contradict himself.

Even if it were true that everyone always does what he thinks is right, one could do it only by repressing his awareness of ever doing a wrong, which would amount to the same moral guilt as doing wrong consciously. We cannot help regarding the individual as the same moral agent, whether he acts to repress his consciousness of a wrong act when he commits it, or whether he commits it knowingly. In either case, one is not doing what he really thinks is right, and he is responsible for his action against his own conscience. No one can absolve himself of guilt of an immoral act simply by repressing his consciousness of the fact that it is wrong. Personal autonomy is impossible without honest self-confrontation and self-cooperation. The autonomous man acts basically as a unit, as a whole person, as one whose capacities are concerted and strengthened by inner coherency or integrity. This means that one's conscious and unconscious motives must be at home with each other. It is a psychiatric fact that one must avoid repressing his conscience if he is to be truly integrated within himself. Even common sense tells us that something is wrong when we practice conscious hypocrisy. If I correctly read Frankena, he is telling us that conscious hypocrisy is impossible. I can only ask him: Have you never at the time you were doing something felt that it was wrong? If he answered no, this would seem very odd indeed. My position is this: any human being can be perverse knowingly, and he can enjoy his perversion. One can freely and deliberately act on a less constructive alternative and feel pleasure in doing it, even though he knows in his conscience at the time that it is perverse.

It is not my intention to suggest that human beings can always act in the most constructive possible ways. I am not saying that any human can always do what is objectively right. To expect this from anyone would be totally unrealistic, simply because it is impossible that one can always know exactly what is right. However, it certainly is possible that one can always do what he *thinks* is right. And this, I submit, is the only ideal which we can reasonably expect one another to try to practice consistently. Even here we must have a proviso, namely, that the individual be allowed the prerogative of honest confusion, i.e., those occasions when he is unable to decide clearly even what he *thinks* is right. It is a very naïve error to equate the person with integrity with the person who acts in the most constructive possible way. Integrity does not mean always doing what is right. It means always doing what, to the best of one's ability, one can honestly *discern* to be right.

There is no one among us who exemplifies constant and absolute purity of conscience, or total integration of himself. If history has taught us any humbling lesson, it is that purity of heart and mind has never been an absolute accomplishment in the human struggle for spiritual wholeness. No human mortal can escape the finiteness of his insight and power; hence, none of us can ever be flawlessly circumspect and judicious about how to behave. Also, each of us must always grow; or at least, one must grow or else vegetate and regress. If one chooses to grow, he can do so only by suffering within himself the continuous necessity for self-investigation and self-correction as new experiences call for some inner change in his being. Growth means: either one must negate or revise some of his old ideas and feelings that have proved inadequate, or else he must live with the fact that a responsible search for more truth and meaning often is effortful and painful. Moreover, there can be no escape from the reality of freedom. The human being who really lives is continuously tempted. He must continuously choose between the possibilities of responsible and irresponsible acts.

I have said that it is possible for a person always to do what he *thinks* is right. Yet, I have said that it is not possible for him always to be as knowledgeable about moral proprieties as he should like. I do not believe that there is any contradiction here. On the contrary, there is just a moral necessity to understand the error in expecting any human being to behave always with perfect wisdom. In other words, it is very unwise to expect anybody always to be wise. But the fact remains that a person's always doing what he thinks is right is an absolute ideal, toward which we should strive even though it is obvious that none of us ever accomplishes absolute integrity throughout his life. The validity of an ideal is not undermined by the fact that we fall short of consistently accomplishing it. The ideal of integrity is not negated by the fact that we freely choose not always to be consistent. I have said that it is possible for a person always to do what he *thinks* is right. I mean this literally, except on those occasions when he is unable to decide what should be regarded as right—in which case, he has a right to behave impulsively or instinctively, regardless of the possible consequences of his actions. The fact that we do not take consistent advantage of our possibilities for integrity only indicts us; it does not excuse or justify us.

There are mechanistic psychologists who declare this ideal to be false and naïve. They say that humanly unaccomplished ideals are not valid ideals at all. My answer to these psychologists is vehement. They deem themselves realists; whereas in reality they are merely cynical, for they deny that there is any meaningful distinction between the ways in which we behave and the ways in which we can and should behave. Mechanistic psychology reduces man to a machine and denies the reality of choice. It therein also denies that moral responsibility is even theoretically possible. For morally speaking, responsibility depends upon possibility. It is meaningless to say that a person *ought* to do something if it is not possible for him to do it. *Ought* clearly implies *can*. If a person cannot possibly perform an act, there is absolutely no reason why we should say that he *ought* to perform it. Moral responsibility exists only when one has the power either to execute an act or to leave it undone.

This absence of perfect integrity and wisdom in our lives is used by many as an argument against autonomy as an ideal. Such an argument is of course false, for integrity of conscience and action must remain an ideal, simply because of the potency it *can* provide the individual to function as a whole being. Needless to say, this ideal can be freely ignored or neglected by any person who knows of it, but only at the expense of impairing his autonomy.

Today the individual in our culture is frequently pressured to make compromises to group judgment, to conform to prevailing opinion, to "live democratically" by complying with the majority view. One often is urged to be "cooperative," "a good team worker," "a regular guy," "a well-adjusted man," to find happiness in being "well rounded," to "get along well with others," etc. Social critics such as Riesman, Whyte, Wilson, and Sykes accuse the masses of making so many unjustifiable social compromises that their lives are insipid. Psychologists such as May and Fromm describe the morbid symptoms of character sickness that result whenever these compromises are made. Existentialist philosophers (Sartre, Heidegger, *et al.*) censure the general conduct of the masses as basically "inauthentic," as devoid of the courage for self-projection and the will to "be." I find the generally disparaging picture of humanity these critics portray to be slightly self-righteous and exaggerated, yet basically accurate. In truth, the majority of my colleagues in most of the institutions where I have worked, have indeed been unwilling to stand up and fight to change situations about which they bitterly complain in private, but never out in the open where consequences have to be suffered. In my mind, there is no doubt that the individual who will "stick out his neck" and face great risks in behalf of truth for its own sake is definitely a member of a small minority of the human race. Nor is one likely to find a more widespread presence of true character or integrity in the deviant groups, such as the hippies, beatniks, and gangs.

I have already indicated that my concern in this book is to present a body of principles which can help the individual avoid the loss of his self in the whirlpool of unjustifiable social pressures and demands. With regard to my first principle, many questions naturally arise. Therefore, it is essential to achieve a clear conception of moral guilt, and I shall attempt this with the following points:

1. A person may imagine that he has caused some harm which in reality he has not caused. This is *false* subjective guilt.

2. One may cause harm and acknowledge it, and feel sorry for it, and this is *true* subjective guilt.

3. The individual is responsible for anything that he does, in the sense that he is the agent who acts, and is objectively guilty of any harm which he is the strict cause of, whether or not he acknowledges it to himself.

4. However, objective guilt is not necessarily moral guilt. Neither is subjective guilt necessarily moral guilt, regardless of whether it is true or false. For there are two kinds of guilt, namely, moral and mischance.

5. Moral guilt consists in knowingly and deliberately harming oneself or another, needlessly. However, since self-deception is possible, moral guilt also consists in doing needless harm while repressing one's consciousness of the wrongness of the act, and rationalizing it as right.

6. Willful ignorance is often wrong. One is morally guilty if he does needless harm which he could have avoided, had he not been willfully ignorant. To deny this is to sanction any kind of harm or tragedy that is caused by willful ignorance, self-complacency, laziness, conceit, or ill will. If one has had

an opportunity to learn right from wrong but has freely chosen not to, then his willful ignorance is clearly irresponsible.

7. Everyone has a right to err, to be wrong, to cause harm accidentally, and be the subject of no moral guilt insofar as he causes harm because he has had no opportunity to learn better. When judging himself or others, the mature person will stop to consider that there may be extenuating circumstances for the causes of a harmful act. The appearance of moral guilt may not at all represent moral guilt genuinely.

8. Everyone has a right to do knowingly any wrong, provided he is willing to accept all the consequences and is capable of redressing all the wrong that he has done, in its complete breadth and depth. Otherwise, why should we be free? If this were not the case, then what ontological basis or rationale could there be for our moral freedom? How could moral dignity be possible if we were not free to act in undignified or immoral ways? Yet, what moral logic could there be to our freedom if we were permitted to act immorally without any obligation to accept the consequences, and have no ultimate retribution necessarily in store for us? I cannot offer proof that in the order of nature there is any ultimate, long-range justice, retribution, or moral logic. However, it is obvious that if this is not the case, all talk of moral truth and responsibility is purely arbitrary and nonsensical.

9. If a person honestly thinks that it is wrong to act on alternative number one, and right (or less wrong) to act on alternative number two, then he is contradicting himself if he acts on alternative one, regardless of whether he admits it or denies it through a repression of his conscience. For in this case, he is acting as though a wrong were a right and a right were a wrong, which is logically outrageous. One need not be a psychiatrist to know that such self-contradictory behavior is emotionally untenable. It splits the feeling person into incompatible forces which tend to breed neurosis. Ordinarily, we call such an inconsistent action hypocrisy. The logician would prefer to label it a "paralogism," which is the employment of a valid principle of reason to deny the very validity of the selfsame principle. Or more precisely with regard to morality,

it is the use of the principle of distinction between right and wrong to negate any meaning in the distinction itself. It is simply illogical to say that the right thing to do is the wrong thing to do (although one can logically distinguish between wrong and less wrong, or between right and less right).

If the individual contradicts himself in this manner often enough, he may become neurotic or psychotic. In doing what he really thinks is wrong for no reason other than to feel safe or socially accepted, he sets himself against himself and betrays his own schemata for authentic existence. This is true regardless of whether his self-contradiction is an instance of conscious ("honest") sin or unconscious self-deception. In either case, the individual kills his own conscience. He acts as though he had sold his belief in his own mind and heart. He divides himself against himself, thus weakening his power for effective action in both his public and private life. If he contradicts himself often enough about things that really matter to him, he may go insane. I am not prepared to concede that anyone may *completely* lose contact with himself by splitting himself entirely in two. This would deny that a human being is essentially one agent, ultimately responsible for the diversity of effects he may create within himself. However, there is no doubt that a free agent can so shatter his own integrity of personality that it becomes extremely difficult for him to repair it, even with the most competent psychiatric aid.

10. It often is necessary to make compromises in life, out of practical necessity. However, one must continually examine himself critically to make certain that his compromises are intelligent and morally justifiable. A justifiable compromise consists in denying one principle or value in order to honor a yet higher principle or value. For example, an innocent pauper may think that it is generally wrong to steal, yet realize that under certain circumstances he has a moral responsibility to steal—to wit, when he honestly cannot succeed in finding gainful employment and must steal from the stingy rich in order to feed his hungry wife and children. In this case, he must choose between stealing and neglecting his family's need for food. His principle of responsibility to his family overrides the principle

of not stealing from the rich, when acting on the former does more good and less harm than acting on the latter.

11. An unjustifiable compromise consists in betraying a higher principle or value for a lower one, out of cowardice or selfishness.

12. Every individual has the right to confusion when confronted with any situation in which he does not know (or honestly believes that he does not know) the right way to act. When he is forced to decide but cannot see a basis for a morally right decision, then he must enjoy the right of risk, the right to a sense of innocence if in his blind action he hurts either himself or others. In fine, anyone under such circumstances has a right to disappoint society, to hurt both himself and others, and in so doing be inculpable if his motives are good and he is willing to do whatever he can to reconstruct all the wreckage he discovers he has done in ignorance.

In this ethic of autonomy, the first principle assumes that no one can be true to society unless he is first true to himself. The individual must realize that he cannot enjoy genuine social togetherness unless first he is together with himself. Of course, I cannot claim to be offering any new insight here. I have discussed the need for freedom and integrity of conscience only to elaborate an already known truth, not to claim the invention of a new principle. Literally, it goes back to Shakespeare, who said in *Hamlet*: "This above all: to thine own self be true, and it must follow, as the night the day, thou canst not then be false to any man." In fact, the principle can be traced to Socrates' famous adage, "Nosce te ipsum."[2]

I am not allowing that objective right and wrong are invented by man. That there can be no moral truths except those which each individual invents for himself, hence no objective morality whatever, is the nihilistic error of contemporary existentialism and pragmatism. Herein, I have argued consistently that if there are no moral truths that transcend the arbitrary willfulness of men, there can be no objective morality possible. What I am saying is simply this: every individual's conscience develops in its own peculiar social milieu and set of circumstances, and no intelligent theory of morality can ignore this indisputable fact. Each individual's conscience has its origin in the context of his own ego development, his own unique history of personal experiences, and his own unique hereditary nature in combination with the many influences of his unique environment. I have strenuously objected to nihilistic doctrines which deny that there are universal moral laws and ideals. Every individual's experience differs in some degree from others', with regard to his opportunity and *capacity* to *discover* what these moral laws and ideals are. Moreover, every individual's disposition or willingness to learn is at least in some respects unique. Certainly, an isolated primitive cannibal cannot be expected to know as much about morality as persons of greater wealth and culture who have had more opportunity to learn. *There is no individual, in any society or in any time, who can afford to be without integrity,* and this includes the ignorant cannibal precisely as much as it does the pope in Rome. There is not now, there never has been, and there never will be a society endowed with the right to abuse, ignore, or destroy the integrity and freedom of conscience of any of its individual members. No individual can be as healthy without integrity as he can be with it; nor can any society which ignores this principle be as beneficial for its members as it would be if it recognized the validity of the principle and honored it. Whenever people ignore or abuse this principle in human relations, the inevitable results are anarchy, tyranny, and terror.

There are indeed universal truths. One of the most important is the fact that every individual should enjoy the right and liberty to work out his own salvation. In spite of how sincerely one may believe in the objectivity of moral law or truth, and in the existence of God as the ultimate ground and arbiter of right from wrong, the fact remains that every individual must through the light of his own reason and conscience discern what that truth is. Everyone must assess truth from the standpoint of his own individual experience and must suffer any and all the consequences of his decisions regarding right and wrong. Indeed, how could it possibly be otherwise? In his limited wisdom, can any human being ever know the truth quite as fully as God knows it? Obviously, everyone must discern right and wrong with the risks and inevitable faultiness of his own finite human capacities. Any allegiance he may have to God must be in and through his allegiance to his own integrity of conscience. For him, his own conscience must be the ultimate authority because if he is not true to himself, then certainly he cannot be true to God. Even if his conscience is objectively wrong, because it is oriented around principles and values that are objectively false, he always has the right to be wrong as long as he lacks the opportunity or capacity to learn better. After all, what else but one's own conscience can be one's guide? Certainly, no one can orient his life to principles and values of which he has had no experience. One can attempt to discern the will of God only through the laborings of his own mind, his own heart. After listening openly to others, one must then listen to his own voice, to his own honest evaluation of what all the others have said. Then, he must obey his own voice. Of course, he may freely choose not to do this. But let one fact be unmistakably clear: the moment a man muffles his own voice he sells his soul. He becomes a pebble or a piece of clay. In fact, he becomes infinitely lower than these things, for a pebble or a piece of clay can have no capacity to choose, hence no moral responsibility.

I should recommend that religious authoritarians read the book by the great German theologian Dietrich Bonhoeffer titled *Ethics*.[3] Here, I wish to express agreement with Bonhoeffer's belief that we can seldom, if ever, know the will of God with altogether the same clarity that God himself knows it. Indeed, to equate our own wisdom with his can be naïve and dangerous. To do so would be to say that our own moral knowledge and judgment are complete, and this is blasphemously conceited. In liberal Protestant theology, it is generally regarded as a sin to identify one's own moral judgment or understanding with that of God.

Even so, I think we would be foolish to believe that we are deprived of any capacity to know universal moral truths simply because we are born with finite minds. The fact that we cannot know all that God knows is no argument that we can never know anything at all for certain. I grow impatient with theologians like Fletcher (*Situation Ethics*) who talk as though a human being must understand everything, or else he cannot definitely and clearly understand anything. I cannot believe that a good and wise God would create children who could never know anything whatever for certain. The belief that God has done this seems to me to be the attitude toward him that is most nearly blasphemous, since it does an injustice to him.

It has been objected, "But how can you grant freedom of conscience to children, whose egocentrism would make them diabolically dangerous if they were not arbitrarily restricted and disciplined?" My answer to this is threefold:

1. Children *must* be disciplined to understand the principles of this ethic, that they cannot encroach upon the rights of others without losing these rights in themselves. A child must be made to understand that he does not deserve freedom and integrity of his own conscience if he violates it in others.

2. No child whose need for integrity is stymied can be as healthy, happy, and loving as he would be if this need in him were fulfilled. Wise parents will honor this need in their children by giving them cogent, plausible reasons for doing the things they require of them to do. Of course, children sometimes are indisposed to appreciate reason, no matter how sound and friendly it might be. When this happens, as it often does at certain age levels, children must not be permitted to violate the rights of others with impunity.

3. The cultivation of freedom and integrity of conscience in a child is indispensable to both his own welfare and that of those around him. This is true for the simple reason that a child, like any adolescent or adult, without integrity cannot be trusted and will be a continuous problem both to himself and to others.

Also, it has been objected, "But wasn't Hitler following his own conscience, always doing what *he* thought was right?"

The psychiatric writings I have read regarding Hitler's personality seem to agree unanimously that he was a highly neurotic person, characterized by an inordinate amount of self-deception, self-contradiction, and corruption of conscience. Summarily, he can hardly be used as an argument to prove that integrity is not an intrinsic value. On the contrary, Hitler's evil actions grew largely out of the fact that he was a highly frustrated and self-mutilated individual. He suffered those tensions and delusions that are found only in persons marked by a great corruption and dissatisfaction of the primordial need for integrity.

7.

Some Ground to Stand On

My SECOND principle also is not new. I have found it grounded in the hoary historical wisdom of mankind as well as in the findings of modern philosophical psychology. It is for obvious reasons that I have labeled it the "principle of earnestness," since it states that *one should always act to make his life as beautiful, meaningful, and valuable as possible.*

This principle is necessitated by the very definition which I have given to autonomy. The reason for any individual's existence should be to get as much good out of living and to put as much into it as possible. It might be objected that this is a trite observation. It might be said that I am verbalizing commonsense knowledge, which is a poor excuse for taking up the pages of a book. I should readily admit that this is ancient, pristine wisdom, that it is nothing which has been discovered by modern psychology or philosophy. However, the idea that people are generally conscious of the validity of this principle, or that they usually put it into practice, is unquestionably false and is itself evidence of the spiritual inertia of the majority of humanity in any age. I am convinced that few people go through life conscious of this fact even half the time. The sad truth is that our culture is sick with masses of people who practically never go beyond half-living. In our wretched lukewarmness and lazy complacency we spend half our effort trying to avoid really great living. We half-work, half-learn, half-love, and even half-play. That this is true not only of the present generation but of all others has been the outstanding complaint of all great religious leaders, philosophers, and social critics of all cultures and times. The inertia of the masses is not a condition peculiar to American culture; it is found everywhere, indeed in many societies much more than in our own. I have lived eleven years in twenty-one countries and everywhere have found a common absence of high-mindedness or an obsession for great living. Do we need evidence that most of us are poorly skilled, and poorly motivated, at living authentically and deeply?

The average person's life revolves around a general routine, complacency, and ordinariness. Superficiality pervades our intellectual and artistic life, as well as our moral life. Until the individual fully realizes the validity of the principle of earnestness and decides to act it out in his daily life, he will cheat both himself and society. A genuine ethic of autonomy must hold to the highest ideals and tax the individual with the most noble challenge to a rich life. The validity and importance of this principle need only to be recalled, not defended. We find it crucial in the teachings of Jesus, who said he wanted to make our lives more abundant. It is eminent in the philosophy and psychology of all the great thinkers. Curiously enough, we find it even in the preaching of the nihilists, for example, Nietzsche, Sartre, and Camus, who have insisted that there are no universal or absolute truths, no values that endure throughout time, yet have invariably contradicted themselves when forced to face naked moral realities.

In his *Myth of Sisyphus,* Camus declares categorically that all existence is absurd. He tells us that human heroism can consist only in facing the truth that our lives are ultimately without any rationale or hope. The only real philosophical question is: Since life is absurd, should I, or should I not, commit suicide? In *The Rebel,* Camus describes heroism as the will to rebel, to reject suicide, to refuse to run away from absurdity in any way. Life is essentially meaningless and futile, yet one must obstinately will to exist and to be happy, while remaining fully conscious of the fact that it is absurd to remain alive. To seek consolation in belief in God or in the immortality of the soul is unrealistic and unmanly. There can be no ground for hope, and for this reason there can be no justification for hope in "this insane world." Admitting that his doctrine of absurdity is itself absurd, Camus insists that this is just the way things are. He objects to suicide on the grounds that it is a retreat from the "truth." The true philosopher is a rebel; he decides to live with absurdity, rather than to escape from it by taking his life. That all human existence is futile is the *truth,* and it is with this truth that we should be willing to live. The anti-hero is the nonrebel, i.e., he would escape from absurdity through suicide or religious faith. For anything to exist at all is inherently absurd, and there is no possible way to undo this fact. Therefore, to seek a solution in religious illusion (or in suicide, which would solve the problem simply by putting an end to it) is to falsify the truth of absurdity, hence also to falsify and negate oneself. Only after we accept absurdity and decide to live with it can we exist authentically and have true dignity. Only then does the "body, compassion, the created world, action, human nobility . . . resume their place in this insane world. Man will find again the wine of absurdity and the bread of indifference which nourish his greatness."[1]

In reading Camus, one readily notes that he has an emotional *preference* for the absurd. He has an enthusiasm for keeping his experience of it alive, by denying that there are any intellectual or philosophical solutions possible. That he personally wants existence to be absurd is obvious in his systematic resistance to all attempts at solving the problem rationally. By an under-the-table twist in the rules of logic, he asks us to accept his rejection of reason as "the truth" about reason. Just *ad hominem,* he becomes the rational man in what he insists is an irrational world. For him, there is only one objective truth, namely, that any objective criteria for rational thinking are inherently impossible. It is not my purpose to cover all of them here, but there are numerous objections to this nihilist attempt to make absurdity intelligible. There simply can be no way to show rationally that there is no rationality in the world. The man who employs universal principles to undermine the selfsame principles obviously is resorting to trickery.

In *The Rebel,* Camus attacks nihilism and objects to the accusation that he himself is a nihilist. But like all nihilists, who unconsciously presuppose objective criteria and values while consciously denying them, he merely exemplifies the self-contradiction of the rebel who has no valid reasons to rebel. First, he categorically renounces universal or eternal truths and values. He attacks all absolutes on the basis that they lead to enslavement, terror, tyranny, and murder. He attacks the false absolutes of the nazi Germans, the Marxist Communists, the Catholic Inquisition, and other despotic historical powers. But then, he betrays the absurdity of his own insistence on absurdity, his notion that a human being can "nourish his greatness" on nothing other than the "wine of absurdity and the bread of indifference." Like all nihilists, Camus criticizes those human actions in the world which he finds to be evil; but in doing this, he inevitably appeals to some values and principles that are objectively valid. Before he knows it (in fact, he never becomes conscious of it at all), he does a philosophical about-face and talks like a realist. We find him insisting on "justice," "meaning," and "truth," as though these things are grounded in something more than merely his subjective will. For example, he attacks the tyrannical practices of Hitler, Franco, and Stalin. It is, of course, impossible to criticize cogently other people's actions without appealing to some criteria that are unaffected by changing customs and merely arbitrary judgments. Is it not a simple truth that no moral critic can stand on solid ground unless first there is some solid ground on which to stand?

Both Camus and Sartre are antiabsolutists, yet both vehemently criticize the harmful political and social actions of other people. They accuse each other of contradictions and naïveté, and both unconsciously deviate from their common premise that there are no universal truths. For example, Camus attacks Sartre's existentialism, saying: "If man has no purpose that can be treated as a mark of value, then how can history have a meaning that is discernible here and now? If history has such a meaning, why does man not make *that* his purpose? And if he does so, why does he experience the terrible and unremitting freedom of which you speak?"[2]

It is unfortunate when a sensitive and serious person cannot bring his soul into unity. In simple logic, no one can successfully object to false absolutes without recourse to true ones. In desperation, the nihilist must inevitably turn to some objective meaning, some purpose in history, or else he can turn to nothing at all. The schizophrenic disunity in Camus' moral philosophy is equaled by Sartre's, although the two thinkers express their contradictions with different sentiments and motives. Sartre denies the possibility of any universal truths, yet draws on them to attack his enemies and defend his own position. In fact, he answers Camus in the surprising language of an out-and-out realist. Man, we are told, "participates in history in order to pursue the *eternal*. He uncovers *universal values* in the concrete action which he performs with a specific purpose in view."[3]

I have had lengthy discussions with many nihilists. They talk only a short time before contradicting themselves. There is no avoiding universal truths and values, except by a subjective decision, i.e., when the free individual simply chooses not to face them. But of course, the choice not to face them by no means signifies that they are not really there.

That the principle of earnestness is valid for all men is not subject to a reasonable doubt. It hardly needs proving that the purpose of life should be to live as abundantly as possible. To the extent that any individual fails to do this, he betrays himself and the world. For otherwise, he would be as worthy as possible to himself and to everybody concerned. To be as much of an individual as possible, a man must never cheat himself of any good to which he is morally entitled. Everyone owes to himself the most adventuresome, productive, and beautiful experience of life that his opportunities and endowments permit. That this is the truth is affirmed clearly by both Camus and Sartre in many passages of their otherwise nihilistic writings.

A colleague once objected, "But isn't this principle virtually useless since it is phrased in such ambiguous terms? You speak of 'beautiful,' 'meaningful,' and 'valuable.' But aren't these terms extremely vague, imprecise, and often personal?"

Granted, these terms can never be perfectly defined.

I certainly am not saying that all persons can go through life always experiencing precisely the *same* beauties, meanings, and values, although it seems obvious that communication with one another is impossible except when we can experience meanings and values in common. The fact that we do not always share the same experiences of beauty does not constitute an argument against the validity of this principle. The most beautiful music some persons can appreciate or produce is that of the harp, but for others it is that of the violin, etc. I express myself most creatively with a piano, and my neighbor does it with a horn. It is obvious that everyone has some experiences of beauty and value that are unique and private, which is precisely as it should be. Otherwise, how could we even refer to anyone as an *individual?* There are innumerable different kinds of beauty, both possible and actual, and no one of us can appreciate or create all of them. In varying degrees, everyone differs in his talents and the ways in which he has acted to develop them.

8.

To Judge Fairly

I HAVE LABELED the third principle the "principle of equity," because it states that *everyone should be self-reflective, should judge himself as cautiously and critically as possible, and should judge others by the same criteria with which he judges himself under the same circumstances.*

It cannot reasonably be doubted that every person in every society needs freedom and integrity of conscience. However, it is no less certain that any individual who always did what he thought was right but ignored the principle of equity in human relations would be egocentric and dangerous. The first principle of this ethic might just as well be ignored if it is not to be tempered and enlightened by the other principles which realize and honor the social virtues. As I stated previously, the ethic of autonomy is organic; each of its principles is true and ultimately works successfully only when in cooperation with the others. Without self-discipline and social consciousness, personal freedom is not only dangerous and harmful to others but downright harmful to oneself, and ultimately leads to self-destruction. It is impossible for anyone to truly fulfill his own essential needs without recognizing and honoring the essential needs of others. We have abundant psychiatric and sociological evidence, and we should realize through our common sense,

that self-fulfillment cannot occur in social isolation or aliena-
tion. Anyone claiming a right to self-realization through denying the rights of others is simply immature and stunted.

Like the others, the third principle is not new. It is just primordial, enduring wisdom. It is found most dramatically expressed in the words of Jesus: " 'Judge not, that you be not
judged. For with the judgment you pronounce you will be
judged. . . .' "[1]

This means, if I interpret it correctly, that in judging others
we should leave all finality to God. For the human urge to hate
and to condemn always craves finality in its critical judgment
of others. Certainly, we know that there are no wholly "mature" or "pure" human beings alive, endowed with the right
or power to sentence permanently a fellow human being's destiny. Yet practically, we also know that the admonition not to
judge cannot mean that we must live without ever judging one
another at all. We cannot grow in virtue and understanding
without striving to maintain some valid moral distinctions in
studying and criticizing one another's acts. Probably no man in
the world has a self-image that corresponds quite precisely with
the image that God has of him. What a person actually is in
reality is one thing; what he *thinks* he is, is another. And no
one short of God could ever clearly understand the difference.
No human is ever quite as pure as he thinks he is. Hence ideally,
we should strive to live blamelessly and harmlessly while taking
the position of judging others. It would be unreasonable to assume that *any* judgment of oneself and others is a sin. Only to
judge others self-righteously and to consider oneself insusceptible
to the same criteria—this is wherein the danger lies.

We can have no moral order of any kind without criticism.
Without judgment and counter-judgment, we cannot grow and
can neither cultivate nor demand social virtues and lofty
character. It is not possible for people to live earnestly without
judging, and in judging we can never escape all the risks of possible error and self-righteousness. Since judging is necessary, the
individual must have the courage to judge and to risk error and
guilt. But for the same reason, he must also have the humility
to admit the possibility of self-righteousness and prejudice, and

to reserve any final judgments for God. Let the individual judge, but beware.

Through critical self-reflection, one is able to modify continually his image of himself, and to guard against the kind of self-satisfaction that frustrates his need to change, grow, and become a better person. No one's character is so valuable and beautiful that it cannot become yet more valuable and beautiful; nor is anyone's understanding so great that it does not need to become yet greater. These observations are so clearly established in fact that it may seem to the reader I am didactic in even mentioning them. But if this is the case, then it should seem no less obvious that we do, in reality, very often lose sight of these simple truths.

At the heart of continuous, constructive growth in a person's character there has to be a *habit* of critical self-analysis. Such a habit can be overdone, of course, since life is meant primarily to be lived and only secondarily to be analyzed. But it is unlikely that any of us ever devotes exactly the right amount and proper kind of attention to analyzing himself. Yet, it is essential that all of us try to do this, and that we realize that a valid self-analysis outside the context of our relations with others is impossible. Therefore, the judgment of ourselves and others must be tied together by a common social reality which requires a common social logic. Being "anthropologically minded," or knowing that mores and norms vary from culture to culture, cannot alter the fact that a common principle of equity in human moral evaluation should apply to every individual. No man, in any society, can rightly set himself up as immune by claiming the privilege of a different set of moral criteria for judging himself than for judging others. Of course, we should realize that other persons may have had a different background of moral training than we have had. Consequently, we can hardly expect these persons to behave the same as we do. However, the realization and appreciation of this fact is itself a requirement of the principle of equity. In judging others, one should always give them the benefit of all moral reasonableness if oneself is to deserve a right to such reasonableness. To judge others more leniently (or more harshly) than one judges oneself under the same circumstances is unreasonable and unjust. In a sense, it does not really matter whether a person's unjust act is perpetrated against others, or only against himself; for in either case, the results in the long run are damaging both to the individual and to everyone whom his self-relations eventually affect. Inequity in one's moral judgments and actions impairs the autonomy of the individual and thus cheats both him and all those who need and deserve to be treated justly by him. Inevitably, a man makes enemies of those whom he judges unfairly or differently than he judges himself under the same circumstances. And because relations with enemies are never as fulfilling as relations with friends, any inequity in the individual's judgment can only impede his autonomy.

9.

To Be and Let Be

Coming now to the fourth principle, I submit that its validity is self-evident. Also, I acknowledge that it is not original; it is, on the contrary, simply drawn from the primordial intuition of intrinsic moral truth. The truth of this ideal has been discovered by wise men of every generation for innumerable spans of human history. But of course, the fact that it is self-evident does not mean that its validity is acknowledged by all people in all ages. All of us at times lose sight of this principle, just as we at times deliberately ignore it or abuse it even when we are conscious of its verity. Moreover, there are always nihilists among us who deny that there is any principle grounded in any truth whatever. There are even professional philosophers who insist that nothing is inherently true or false, that the term "truth" can have no objective philosophical meaning. I have already criticized this position in the first part of my book and now appeal to common sense and to logical reason.

With this principle, I state that all moral rights are bilateral in nature. Or to put it again precisely: *Every individual has the right to creative and independent thinking and acting as long as he honors this same right in all others, and as long as in his differences he does not inflict needless harm or suffering on himself or others.*

Surely the reader will not require proof that there is much needless suffering and harm in the world. We often have difficulties trying to discern necessary from unnecessary suffering. To avoid inflicting needless suffering, we must be very cautious in our actions and must face many serious problems. Even as we honor this principle in theory, there often are great difficulties in discovering efficacious ways and means of implementing the ideal in practice. But one thing is certain—no one can feel safe in the presence of a person who never honors this ideal in his treatment of others. Granted all the difficulties in practicing this principle, the fact remains: one is unquestionably a better person when he keeps the ideal in mind and tries to put it into practice.

Certainly no person can have a right to speak if he will not grant this same right to all others who under the same circumstances also honor it. No one has a right to freedom of sin if he will not grant to all others this same right. Nor has anyone a right to freedom of conscience in determining his behavior if he will not let all others who honor this principle enjoy the same. Everyone has a right to freedom of thought and difference of opinion only as long as he respects this same right in all others. The moment he denies this right to any person who honors it, he alienates the right in principle and therefore logically alienates it from himself.

Ignorance of this ideal or indifference to it makes devils of zealots who claim to enjoy special privileges of power and immunity to the logic of moral rights. Such ignorance causes tyrants and bigots to arise and declare: "Mine is the one and only true church. Mine is the one and only true form of government. Mine is the one and only true economic system. The members of my race are superior and must have special licenses and prerogatives. Mine is the one and only correct way to eat, dress, and talk. Only *I* know the right way to get things done. My insights into beauty and art are infallible. Only I, and those like me, can determine true from false, or right from wrong. You are a stupid heretic if you do not believe as I believe. Even if you are sincerely following your conscience and reason to the best of your ability, you are nevertheless a heretic of truth, for you are wrong! I have a right to follow the mandates of my conscience, for I am right. But you do not have this right, for you are wrong."

The unilateralist in rights (such as the foregoing) is never a true individualist, for he is neither just nor rational and would reserve the right to be an individual only to those who are like himself. Only he can be right, and those who are wrong can have no right to be wrong, no matter how sincerely and innocently they come by their ignorance of the truth.

The unilateralist inevitably is thwarted by reality, by the enemies he makes in denying others their rights. People oppose and resent him for arbitrarily setting himself up as better than they, as someone special who would enjoy the despotic privilege of running others down with impunity. But that any despot can indefinitely succeed in doing this is a delusion, for true success in human relations requires reason, humility, and love. No individualism can possibly succeed that does not assess face to face the fact that everyone is only a human being, and all humans are subject to the same laws of logic of moral rights.

Genuine autonomy for the moral unilateralist is altogether impossible, for such a person is governed more by fallacious reason, conceit, and ill will than by awareness of the truth about man. With such unfortunate traits, the selfish individual can only hold himself down because he stands against the needs of humanity.

There can be no plausible objection to this principle. Anyone who would refute it must cut his own throat. The only alternative is a return to the evil of arbitrary and brutal power, which is practically a guarantee of the eventual frustration or destruction of freedom and dignity. We must allow others to be themselves as long as they do not impede our own right to be, as we ourselves wish and choose to be. Admittedly, there is much pain in living by this principle, because it is inevitable that we shall to some extent want others to share our values. We shall want others to hold sacred what we hold sacred, or to choose the same life we choose, insofar as like choices make our daily lives more pleasant and harmonious. There is inescapable anxiety and loneliness in store for parents who allow their children freedom to reach out and choose their own philosophies and ways of life. The teacher who allows students to differ with him, to reject freely his values and beliefs, will know the pain of separation and failure in communication. Yet, one fact is certain: parents and teachers who do not allow their children and students this freedom will encounter more pain and frustration than those who do allow it. For nothing eventually entices a person of character to rebel and explode more certainly than to try to place him in a strait jacket, to suffocate his freedom, to deprive him of his right to be himself. Only cowards submit to unreasonable pressures, and all cowards eventually become cruel. No person can be mistreated without resenting it. Or at least, this is true of people who are rational and sane. Admittedly, there are many who repress their resentment and do not show it outwardly, but this cannot remain indefinitely the case. No one can indefinitely repress the tensions of a mounting hatred of tyranny without eventually exploding, regardless of how fearful he might be of the results of outwardly displaying his feelings.

It has been objected, "But can't this principle be used for evil as well as for good ends? For example, if you allow a student in the classroom to violate parliamentary etiquette in speaking, as long as the same student allows all others to violate it also, then aren't you condoning anarchy and bedlam, out and out?"

My answer to this objection has come through the enlightening experience of much time in the classroom. First, I simply do not condone any person's arbitrarily overriding the values of parliamentary etiquette in classroom speech, or in any other public gathering where the chairman is attempting to honor and execute democratic parliamentary procedures. Second, the objection is based on a very unrealistic and false estimation of human nature and behavior, for there is, in fact, no person who arbitrarily violates reasonable rules of parliamentary etiquette and allows all others also to violate them as arbitrarily as they wish. The anarchist inevitably contradicts himself. When the pains and disadvantages of lawlessness begin to outweigh the advantages, he invariably switches his position and demands the recognition of certain principles and order. Fascists, Communists, and nihilists invariably cry out for recognition of their "rights" when they themselves become the victims of their own brand of intellectual arbitrariness and political tyranny.

10.

Oneself a Person

ACCORDING to the principle of ward, *every just individual has the right and duty to defend himself and others from any form of tyranny or injustice, insofar as he is capable.*

I regard this maxim as in no need of proof. Certainly, no person who treats others reasonably and morally at all times deserves to be treated unjustly. None of us is always consistently rational in his reasoning and just in his actions. However, the truth of this principle is in no way affected by the fact that we do not always realize it or choose to live by it. There is no conceivable refutation of the moral right of the just person to defend himself against unreasonable treatment. In fact, the just man has not only the right to defend himself against injustice but also the duty. For obviously, if he will not defend himself from harm to the extent of his worth and capacity, then he is perpetrating an injustice against himself; hence, he is not in the first place a truly just man.

In the ethic of autonomy, it is essential to recognize and honor the fact that oneself is a person as much as anyone else; and that, for this reason, one should be equally the subject and object of only just thoughts and actions at all times. He who considers himself moral but will not defend himself against the immoral actions of others, contradicts himself by making himself the object of their injustice—which is no less a crime than for oneself to commit an injustice against another. In fact, such cowardice or masochistic thinking is a crime against humanity because it teaches a lesson in false humility rather than manly humility. It sets an erroneous example of justice and publicly condones or tolerates evil. There is no essential moral difference in allowing oneself to be the object of evil than in allowing it for others.

I think that we should qualify the principle of ward in one respect. I have stated that the just individual has the duty to defend *others* from any form of injustice or tyranny. With regard to helping others, there is admittedly a special problem, namely, how to help others when they do not deserve to be helped, or when they themselves freely choose to be both the subjects and the objects of their own evil acts. In trying to help those unwilling to help themselves, there are serious problems indeed. For example, we may have no right to help others if trying to help them would obstruct their freedom to make knowledgeable choices. A wise parent would act unhesitatingly to prevent his child from harming himself in ignorance. However, once a child has grown to possess an understanding of right from wrong (with regard to particular acts), there surely must be limits to anyone's right to interfere with his free management of his own life. The question is, While honoring the principle of freedom of choice in self-determination, to what extent, and under what circumstances, may we rightly act to prevent the other person from hurting himself?

A whole book could be devoted to the analysis and solution of moral problems rising out of concern for those who do not want to be the object of our concern. For reasons of time and space, I cannot deal with such problems here. Suffice it to say, in this regard, that the fifth precept must be applied with great discretion and caution. It is obvious that a person cannot hurt himself without also in some sense hurting all those who are affected by his existence and actions. For this reason (aside from love and care for the person himself), we have a right and duty to interfere in his life. However, there is a stopping point, and I believe it should be *when we see that we would cause more harm by interfering than by simply letting things go.* For example, I have a friend who is killing himself from smoking cigarettes. He is allergic to tobacco and suffers a variety of obvious symptoms. This undoubtedly will shorten his life; it will leave his wife and children without his financial help and love. Even so, we have learned never to talk to him about it for the simple reason that he is unpersuadable and so resentful at any interference in his actions (however well motivated and friendly he finds them) that any attempts to help only create more problems than they solve. It is like the act of prohibition, which would save all men, against their will, from the evils of excess imbibing. Less evil results when we simply allow men to drink.

11.

The Bread of Care

ALTHOUGH I am fully conscious that it will be an offense to the atheist, I submit the sixth principle as essential and absolute. According to this maxim, *the individual should respect and love himself as much as possible, and also respect and love God and his neighbors as much as possible.* This may seem to be an evident truth to many readers. To many others it will seem unrealistic, sentimental, and childish, for there is certainly no need of proof that the notion of love is looked upon with contempt by many persons in this world. Also, there are many who would readily accept the maxim as true but only with the proviso that the word "God" be stricken from it. In insisting that one should love God to enhance his autonomy, I shall be accused by many of begging the question of his existence, of being intellectually "unsophisticated," and of trying to move morality in the direction of fantasy or sentimental delusion. I will write later about the cadaverous humanism of those who claim to love man while despising or rejecting God. But presently, I wish only to remark on the spirit of love in general, which I believe must serve as the foundation and superstructure of the whole ethic and rationale of autonomy.

This maxim is ancient. It stands in the very forefront of the teachings of Jesus, who is the most insightful and influential Person in human history. This principle has been elaborately analyzed in the writings of many modern psychologists, e.g., most recently in the widely selling little book of Erich Fromm, *The Art of Loving*.[1] Also, it is the leading principle in the philosophical psychotherapy of such great analysts as Rollo May, Viktor Frankl, and Paul Tournier. Perhaps I ought once again to state that I am dealing here with an ideal principle. Like the other maxims, this one states what *ought* to be the truth about man and his relations, rather than how we actually choose to behave. I think any philosopher, except for a few insane ones, would insist that all men have a need for a richer and wiser love. Nonetheless, one can hardly overlook the fact that man is free and may choose to hate as easily as to love. As a realist, I see the world as dynamically incomplete and imperfect. In a manner of speaking, I see two different worlds: (1) the world as it *is,* and (2) the world as it *can* and *should* be.

The fact that the ideal of love is as hard to act out in our daily lives as it is impossible to refute makes it the supreme challenge, hence a *sine qua non* for genuine autonomy. In *The Art of Loving,* Erich Fromm has shown why the person who does not love and respect himself is incapable of loving and respecting others. Any person who despises himself and will not forgive himself inevitably in his negativism projects his own image into the character of the world and hates it also. He who disrespects himself must believe that he is unlovable and therefore will also believe that others cannot truly love him. Consequently, he can have little incentive to love others and probably will have a miserable conception of even the love of God.

Fromm's insight into love is brilliant and very interesting. It is unfortunate, however, that he rejects God as a loving Person. It is obvious that he looks upon God as an impersonal abstraction, as only the unconscious forces that constitute the entelechy of the universe. I am quite certain that Fromm would fail to understand me if I tried to communicate to him that I never discovered the richest possibilities of love until I learned to relate with God as a caring Person. I believe that in his analysis of the psychology of love, Fromm approaches the subject entirely too coldly. He fails to realize that a personal relationship with God offers infinitely richer possibilities than a relationship with mere impersonal forces. Moreover, it is entirely too easy for psychologists to become intellectually erudite about the nature of love, so that they may write brilliant and beautiful essays on the subject yet convince hardly anyone that they ever deeply feel it. I agree with Fletcher (pragmatist) that love must be intelligent, well advised, and even cunning in order to be truly responsible. However, I see no point in these things when there is no real *feeling* of the other person's presence and importance. When there is no real desire to relate with another personally, then one's love for him is essentially only barren duty. But here, I am making only a statement of my belief; I do not wish to suggest that Fletcher is not in agreement with it.

I once attended a seminar with a professor whose expertise on the subject of love is world renowned. It happened that there were only twelve students in the class, so that close personal relations and discussions between us were both opportune and essential. Nevertheless, the so-called seminar turned out to be only a monotonous monologue, a series of dry, abstract lectures on the academic questions of love. Not only did the professor show an utter intolerance toward personal dialogue or discussion, but throughout the entire course he did not learn any of our names. In each class session I sat immediately in front of him, right under his nose. Yet, I always felt that he was imprisoned in the shell of his own egocentric thought and being. While pontificating daily on the logic and essences of love, he never once *saw* me, or *heard* me, or showed any evidence that he felt my existence as a person was important.

According to his precepts, "The best life is one in which the individual acts out the most productive and meaningful experience of love possible."

About any philosopher will agree with this in principle, even those who never *feel* such love, either for other persons or for the beauties of nature. Certainly, any person who has known love's beauty and blessings will not doubt that this principle is true. No ethic of autonomy can do the individual justice if it does not bind him with the responsibility to care. All the philosophical psychologists worth mentioning agree that everyone should care greatly for himself and others, and for truth, beauty, and goodness. No person's autonomy can be any greater than his experience of discovery in the pursuit of these things.

Nevertheless, the fact always remains that the individual is free to choose; he does not have to care. Or rather, he has to care only if he chooses to exist authentically. What is more, it is only the ever-present possibility that he can choose inauthentic existence that makes his authentic living really meaningful. If one but chooses to do so, one may care more for paltry comfort and security than for the risks and pain of the great life. One may settle in a spiritual half-heartedness and carefully avoid any great care for anything at all. What, indeed, is easier than to deceive ourselves, to pretend that we really love one another and our neighbors, whereas in truth our care often is more imaginary and shallow than it is passionate and real. Moreover, is it not often merely a feeling of duty, i.e., nothing more than the dry expression of an abstract conception of right and wrong?

Is it not obvious that one should affirm life with his whole heart and mind? There is no questioning this ideal, that we should care deeply and responsibly—but do we *really* know this, even half the time? Today there is much literature on the market describing the forces that would water down the individual's care, distort his character, and sap his energy. The crucial external enemies that we must fight have been described by many writers. Among these enemies are: pressures to submit to vapid conformity; the imperialism of technology and a machine culture; the false public-relations philosophy of overorganized, mercenary organizations; pressures of outmoded mores and customs; the tyranny of fashions and social arbitrariness; and the confusion of the world's highly pluralistic, rapidly changing (sometimes upheaving) social order.

More important, however, are the *internal* enemies and challenges which, for purposes of personal autonomy, must be the ultimate objects of our concern. That we often ignore the challenge of our ideals is common knowledge, even if we usually attribute our abuses of them only to other persons. On this score, we have only to gain from probing and exposing each other's hypocrisies and faults, provided that we do not do it with a callousness and cynicism that make moral growth and lucidity impossible. We must not accept any philosophy that does a human being the injustice of reducing his importance. Granted, human history often is a study in deception, meanness, cheapness, and morbidity. This can give us no excuse for callousness, for a cynical hopelessness about the individual person and his future. For it must also be granted that history is a study in great aspirations, heroic striving, and sensitive love. It is only upon man's positive possibilities that the true spirit of autonomy can thrive. This means we must allow no thing, no person, and no idea to diminish our feeling of the eternal importance of a human being's life. Today no one is as likely to win a Nobel Prize as the cynical philosopher-writer who, with the most eloquent phrases, wishes to propagate his own demonic despair. Russell, Sartre, and Camus speak to us of "heroism," "authenticity," and "the importance of man." Yet, with nothing short of vehement passion they insist that all reality is hopeless, that a human being's life is an ultimately useless and unimportant flicker in an insane universe that mocks all values.

In the context of this insanity, however, Camus nevertheless tells us:

I have chosen *justice* . . . so as to keep faith with the earth. I continue to believe that this world has no supernatural meaning. But I know that something in the world has meaning—man—because he is the only being who demands meaning for himself. This world at least contains the *truth* of *man,* and our task is to *justify* him in the face of destiny itself.[2]

Here, is there not a fundamental abuse of logic in the attempt to combine nihilism with moralism? Camus first insists that *all* existence is absurd, which would make any "truth" about man logically or essentially impossible. He tells us that "this world is insane," that the only truth is absurdity, and that genuine happiness can be "nourished" only on "the wine of absurdity and the bread of indifference." True happiness is available only to the pessimist, the defiant rebel who obstinately persists in living in spite of his knowledge that his life is an absurd and futile passion.

In *The Myth of Sisyphus,* Camus belabors absurdity almost as an obsession. In fact, he attempts to elevate it to that which is most rational and noble. Philosophical "lucidity," he says, can consist only in a radical affirmation of the fact that human existence is absurd. Our experiences of boredom, loss, contradiction, dereliction, and death prove that there is no God. Human science and logic afford us no explanation whatever of the world. There is no God who can explain life; nor is there any foundation for hope, since there are no abiding reasons and values. Therefore, man must live solely for the sake of expressing his will, his defiant determination to be happy in a world where happiness is logically impossible. Man's absurdity is his only "truth," the only thing to which he can legitimately cling. We acquire philosophical "lucidity" only when we decide to accept and live with this fact. The lucid man is he who creates within his own spirit that obstinate happiness which refuses both suicide and false hope.

Earlier, I pointed to a contradiction in Camus' insistence that no logical solution to the absurd is possible. His dogmatic position that no solution is possible is clearly irrational, for a variety of reasons. First, it is a blunder of the first order to employ logic in an effort to prove that no logic can be validly employed. It makes no sense to argue that the world can make no sense. Second, Camus is begging the question in insisting that God is impossible. How could he in any way make a cogent judgment on such a question if he were consistent with his original premise that all human judgments (and consequently his own) are arbitrary and absurd? Like Sartre, Camus is unaware of the thetic character of his unbelief. He is by emotional disposition an atheist and takes entirely for granted that the nonexistence of God is an established fact. As a matter of simple fact, it is absolutely impossible to prove that God does not exist. In this respect, Camus' position is grounded purely in personal choice, rather than in any evidence or logic. For to make a logical case for or against anything, one has to presuppose a fundamentally rational world order in which it is possible to make objectively valid distinctions between true and false, factual and nonfactual, and right and wrong judgments. Having already insisted that such distinctions are impossible, Camus succeeds only in vitiating his own reasoning; or else, by a distortion of logic characteristic of the nihilist, he appeals to transcendental values and truths which clearly discredit his own definition and conception of "lucidity." There is something essentially imbecilic in trying to deduce moral values from the absurd, while the absurd, by definition, makes all objective moral distinctions impossible. Finally, Camus' argument is frustrating because it is so roundabout and underhanded. I object to his negativism, which he attempts by logical slight-of-hand to turn into a positive philosophy about man and his future.

On his premises of absurdity, what can he mean when he says, "I have chosen *justice*, so as to keep faith with the earth"? How can there be any valid criterion of justice, or injustice, in a totally "insane world"? What can he mean about man when he tells us that "our task is to justify him in the face of destiny itself"? If man's existence is absurd, and if his certain destiny is annihilation, then how can anyone "justify" a life that is essentially and categorically unjustifiable? Why not, in this case, just agree with Sartre's attitude that "man is a useless passion," and that, because he is totally contingent, there can be no justification for his existence?[3] If we start with absurdity, then why not conclude with Sartre that "there is no universe other than a human universe, the universe of human subjectivity," and that for man "there is no law-maker other than himself"?[4]

Sartre clearly reduces all values to purely subjective and individual choices. Completely putting aside the objective universe and history, he describes a human being as "nothing else than his plan." A human being "exists only to the extent that he fulfills himself; he is therefore nothing else than the ensemble of his acts, nothing else than his life."[5]

In regard to the justification of human acts, however, if we are looking for moral consistency, we find no more of it in Sartre than in Camus. The tone of his literature as a whole establishes clearly that he is emotionally, dogmatically, and by willful choice an atheist. To any alert reader, there can be no doubt that Sartre does not want God to exist, that he personally prefers him dead. It is a trait common to philosophical nihilists that they want at all cost to oversee God's death, but then publicly to lament it so as to make their negativism seem an intellectual necessity rather than a free choice for which they are personally responsible. Sartre tells us:

> The existentialist . . . thinks it very distressing that God does not exist, because all possibility of finding values in a heaven of ideas disappears along with Him; there can no longer be an *a priori* Good, since there is no infinite and perfect consciousness to think it. Nowhere is it written that the Good exists, that we must be honest, that we must not lie. . . . Indeed, everything is permissible if God does not exist, and as a result *man is forlorn, because neither within him nor without does he find anything to cling to.* . . . In other words, . . . man is free, man is freedom. On the other hand, if God does not exist, we find no values or commands to turn to which legitimize our conduct. So, in the bright realm of values, *we have no excuse behind us, nor justification before us.*[6]

Thus, Sartre plainly wants us to believe that he laments his own atheism, that unfortunately any person who has his eyes open and wants to face reality must accept atheism as an intellectual and moral necessity. He goes on:

> . . . I'm quite vexed that that's the way it is; but if I've discarded God the Father, there has to be someone to invent values. You've got to take things as they are. Moreover, to say that we invent values means nothing else but this: life has no meaning *a priori.* Before you come alive, life is nothing; it's up to you to give it meaning, and *value is nothing else but the meaning that you choose.*[7]

If I interpret this correctly, it means that we can never choose between right and wrong *as such,* since moral values and ideals have no manner or form of objective status before we bring them into being. This is to say, since "value is nothing else but the meaning you choose," all values are purely subjective and arbitrary, or personal. Because "man is freedom" and freedom is nothingness, all values are contingent, that is, purely happenstance and absurd. Because no ideal values whatever are essential, it is not essential that I act in one way rather than in another in order to be a moral and reasonable person. God is nonexistent. The universe is devoid of ideals or reason and purpose. And therefore man, let us lament, is "forlorn, because neither within him nor without does he find anything to cling to."

If this were the truth, I certainly would agree that our human situation is forlorn beyond words, for I cannot imagine any view of life that is more hopelessly irrational and dispiriting. As a matter of simple fact, however, this is a philosophy that no human being can sincerely affirm and choose to go on living. In a previous chapter I accused Sartre of being schizophrenic in his premises, and now I must do it again. For in the same book in which he makes a meaningful use of the term "ought" impossible, he tells us: "For every man, everything happens as if all mankind had its eyes fixed on him and were guiding itself by what he does. And every man *ought* to say to himself, 'Am I really the kind of man who has the *right* to act in such a way that humanity might guide itself by my actions?' "[8]

Here, is not Sartre in opposition to himself? On the one hand, he tells us what "every man *ought* to say to himself," and speaks of the "right" way to act. On the other hand, he insists that there are no a priori values, i.e., values which we *should* choose because they are necessarily right. And no matter how we act, we can have "no excuse behind us, and *no justification before us.*" Is this not saying, in effect, that we can never have the consolation of knowing when we are right, or the wisdom of knowing when we are wrong? Certainly he has put it plainly enough: we are right for no other reason than the fact that we think we are right, and wrong when we think we are wrong. As Sartre has insisted, a human being is "nothing else than his plan." There is no measure of any individual's worth except the individual's opinion of himself. A man is what he thinks he is, and he is not what he thinks he is not. "Not only is man what he conceives himself to be, but he is also only what he wills himself to be. . . .*Man is nothing else but what he makes of himself.*"[9]

First, we are told that "you have to take things as they are," which implies some objective realities that transcend mere fantasy. But then, we are told that "things as they are" are precisely nothing except what we make and imagine them to be. Jean-Paul Sartre is well known for his attacks on his antagonists and opponents. One could hardly count the times when he has demanded that other people *justify* their acts. What right has he to do this when in the same breath he says that we can "find no values or commitments to turn to which legitimize our conduct"? First, he insists that there can be no "justification" for any human act. But then, he proceeds to lash out at his adversaries; he demands that they *justify* their deeds.

As I have insisted already, to build a rational philosophy of autonomy on such subjective premises as these is simply not possible. For the truth is, there can be no cogent reason for despair about the condition of man and his future. Whatever mistakes or crimes we have committed in the past, in the future we shall commit even worse ones if we despair of the eternal importance of a human life. The despair mongers are caught in their own trap. They falsely attribute their own faithlessness to philosophical realism rather than to a willful negativism within their own spirits.

Atheism is a haggard philosophy. It is marked by adolescent whining about the toughness and challenge of life. A bit of old-fashioned wisdom is now needed to save the modern world from its pseudodisillusionment (i.e., not a freedom from illusions so much as a disposition to revolt against the light). We cannot handle life's challenges without unyielding faith and hope. The literature of nihilism has divulged one very important fact, namely, that despairfulness and lovelessness inevitably coincide. Those philosophers who claim to love man while preaching his doom have yet really to taste love's inspiration and promise—or else they have loved but decided to give it up because of its problems and demands. The atheist does not realize, or refuses to realize, love's challenge to faith and its willingness to suffer. For in truth, the man who loves unselfishly will suffer whatever is necessary for his love's sake. It is this love, and it only, that through time can sustain the will to live and to bear up under all life's problems and pains.

Sartre tells us that he is "very distressed that God does not exist." I, for one, do not find this at all convincing. For what betrays his condonance of the despairfulness of atheism is his host of remarks obviously so loveless in character. For example, no person can feel deeply for his fellows and say that "man is a useless passion."[10] I should say that the truth here is quite the contrary; that indeed, only serious and careful love can save human passion from being ultimately useless. It is this love, and it alone, that can uphold the will to live through all life's tribulations and disappointments.

The reasons Sartre offers for being "distressed" about his atheism are actually quite implausible. He objects to God only on the grounds that his existence would shackle our freedom, or else he would make no difference in our daily lives. With regard to God's obstructing our freedom, he says: " . . . I maintain that there is . . . dishonesty if I choose to state that certain values exist prior to me; it is self-contradictory for me to want them and at the same [time] state that they are imposed on me."[11]

On this point, Sartre makes no intelligible argument; he objects to ideals merely on the ground that they would be tyrannical. His arguments reveal a very naïve and illogical misconception of the nature of freedom. For him, a free choice is simply an absurd act out of nothingness, prior to which there are no ideal values or facts in the cosmic order. Can he really be serious, asking us to believe that before he existed there were no values in the world? Clearly, he has said it: "I maintain that there is . . . dishonesty if I choose to state that certain values exist prior to me."

If we are to take him seriously, then his argument drowns in the mud of solipsism. On the other hand, if he means that there were no values in the world before the *first* man existed, his argument is equally unintelligible, for he is still deriving value from nothing. He first tells us that the concept of God is implausible, that God himself could produce no values with freedom. But then, he substitutes *nothingness* in God's place—and leaves us to accept the absurd results as a more rational philosophy of existence! Is Sartre not begging several questions —namely, (1) that the nonexistence of God is a fact, (2) that everything derives from nothing, and (3) that if God existed, he either could not or would not allow his children freedom of choice between values?

Scientifically speaking, I should readily admit that I, too, beg the question about God. I certainly know of no possible scientific way to prove to a resolute doubter that he exists. However, I do know one thing for certain: If Sartre were correct, then the world and all things in it would be grossly absurd, and science would be impossible. According to Sartre, there is no reason or cause for anything to exist. Everything that exists is "just there," or "*de trop.*" This means that all is absolutely contingent and happenstance because all comes from nothing. Consequently, science is impossible because nature simply does not operate in any lawful or ordered way. But if this is the case, then what right has Sartre to claim that his own atheistic judgments are grounded in factuality and logic? Like Nietzsche and Camus, he would have us derive intelligibility from sheer absurdity, which is playing fast and loose with the rules of logic. Such thinking shows no grasp whatever of the simplest principles of rational reason.

Nevertheless, I again admit to begging the question about the existence of God. But since one has to choose which side of the issue to beg, I choose in behalf of the world's making sense. As Sartre himself admits, without God the world can make no sense whatever. The only alternative is nothingness, which obviously makes no sense, but which Sartre has freely chosen to believe while parading his choice in disguise as an intellectual necessity. Here, his abuse of logic comes most clearly into focus. For if all existence is totally contingent, which means that nothing is necessary or essential, then how can he argue that his atheism is an intellectual *necessity?* How can there be any necessity in a world where nothing is necessary? Has he not told us that "contingency is not a delusion, a probability which can be dissipated," but on the contrary, "it is the *absolute,* consequently, the perfect free gift" for man?[12]

Speaking of begging the question, can anyone logically plead for clarity and truth after declaring that such things are essentially impossible? Sartre first insists that he is "absolutely free." But then, he tells us that he would be "dishonest" not to reject God, since he is forced to reject him on the grounds of logical necessity. He first throws out logic, and with it all objective truths or facts about the essential nature of man and the world. But then, he hands us the nonexistence of God as an intellectual *fact*, having nothing to do with our choices or disputes. Thus, once again we have an example of the nihilist pleading for what he denies, that is, the reality of transcendental truths. Sartre wants to be absolutely free, and insists that he is. Yet, he appeals to a "justification," an "excuse" for his own choices or values—the very thing which he has declared to be impossible or ignoble.

I submit that his conception of personal autonomy is irrational and deluded. There can be no absolute freedom, not even in God. A good and rational God would be limited by his own goodness and rationality, and bound by his own love. The argument that we could make no free choices if God existed simply has no force. For if we define the Lord as a Person, with a dynamic, intrapersonal relation with us, then it is unthinkable that he would have created us as automatons or as only a static projection of himself. It is true that I am bound by my belief in God, at least in a sense. For I can choose either to love or not to love him. Indeed, I must do so every moment of the day. But I cannot really choose to love him without therein, at that moment, being bound by this choice, simply because of what the free act of love means and entails. Once I choose to love God sincerely, I therein choose also to be responsible to him, and this responsibility binds me insofar as my choice is real. Insofar as I am bound, albeit by a free choice, my freedom is essentially a structuring of myself by myself. And I claim that, in the case of love for God, this is a liberation and fulfillment of my being instead of a negative and restricting bondage as it is interpreted by Sartre.

Of course, it is true that my love for the Lord restricts my acts. I refrain from doing some things that I would do if I did not love him. But then, is it not a simple fact that all choices are restrictive in this sense? In any instance of choice, the affirmation of one alternative means at that time the renunciation of all the others. For example, in choosing to love God, I rule out for myself certain alternatives which I might act on if I chose not to believe in him. No matter how anyone acts, he restricts his freedom in this sense. In choosing not to believe in God, Sartre restricts his own freedom, his own possibilities of personal expansion in a life of love for him.

Of course, I honor any person's freedom of choice. That a human being does not have to believe in God, and love him, is established both de jure and de facto. My argument is simply this: the freedom of man is much more restricted without God than it would be with him. This is unwittingly admitted in the nihilist's own insistence that man without God is a hapless and doomed accident in an insane world. I believe *there is no necessity whatever for despair,* for this barren faithlessness that betrays a lack of love for man and a beggarly attention to his possibilities in eternity.

Sartre speaks of man's responsibility to man at the same time that his theory would make it categorically impossible. If every individual is "absolutely free," which means that he is totally self-determined, then he is in no way determined or affected by the conduct of other individuals. Now this, I submit, is as antimoral a theory as anyone could espouse; for how, indeed, could I be responsible to other persons if I could in no way determine or condition their feelings and thoughts?

Sartre attempts to prove that God's existence could make no difference in our daily lives. There is a certain truth in this, that people will choose either to have faith or not to have it, whatever the academic arguments may be. However, the atheist is missing the most fundamental value in the whole enterprise of religious faith, namely, the *love* which can be known only by the person who chooses to affirm God and to relate with him seriously. It is altogether unconvincing that Sartre is really "distressed" about his atheism, as he has asked us to believe. Once given his own premise that God does not exist, he in no way laments the following *absence of love for him,* which is the consequence of atheism that is most important in human life. The nihilist obviously does not know the meaning of this love since he never speaks of it except in such ways as to scoff at it and therein show his ignorance of it. Undoubtedly, some persons are conditioned into atheism by the influence of their parents and teachers, etc. But in the case of Sartre, it is evident that he has known the alternative possibility of belief. If he were consistent with his own premises, he would accept responsibility for his choice, rather than attempting to "justify" it on objective grounds which he himself insists cannot exist. From his own premise of absolute freedom, it would follow that he has *chosen* to be an atheist, just *ad arbitrium*. This being the case, why should he disparage the religious choice, i.e., the love for God and the affirmation of the permanent value of man?

The difference that love for God makes is simply itself. There comes a time when words must stop, and they stop after one mentions the uplifting hope and joy. The man who has this joy in his soul feels completely at home in this world, regardless of all the problems and pains in his life. Unlike Sartre, the faithful person cannot regard himself as an inane and useless passion in a nauseous netherworld. On the contrary, he has roots in a divine rationale and purpose, and he is of permanent value.

12.

The Enduring Reliance

TODAY many of the most renowned writers on the subject of autonomy reject God. Usually, they preach that religious belief and love are grounded in escapism and constitute a hindrance to rationality and integrity. According to Camus, Sartre, Fromm, and Russell, no person can become thoroughly autonomous until he unshackles himself of belief in a personal Creator and an immortal soul. The big prize-winning philosophers tell us that we should enjoy happiness, but that the joy of love for God is fraudulent because it is founded on nothing except illusions. According to these men, all the bases for religious belief are negative, namely, fear, insecurity, wishful thinking, and an unwillingness to face and accept reality.

Wherever I have taught, I have heard some of my colleagues argue that the happiness of love for God is merely the happiness of fantasy, for which the really autonomous man can have no license. That is, true autonomy can consist only in that thought and action which rest in empirical evidence, and nothing more.

This atheistic attitude is epitomized in a highly woeful paragraph by Bertrand Russell, whose rhetoric, I think, is much more admirable than his philosophy.

Says he:

That man is the product of causes which had no prevision of the end they were achieving; that his origin, his growth, his hopes and fears, his loves and his beliefs, are but the outcome of accidental

collocations of atoms; that no fire, no heroism, no intensity of
thought and feeling, can preserve an individual life beyond the
grave; that all the labors of the ages, all the devotion, all the inspiration, all the noonday brightness of human genius, are destined to
extinction in the vast death of the solar system, and that the whole
temple of Man's achievement must inevitably be buried beneath
the debris of a universe in ruins—all these things, if not quite beyond dispute, are yet so nearly certain, that no philosophy which rejects them can hope to stand. Only within the scaffolding of these
truths, only on the firm foundation of unyielding despair, can the
human soul's habitation henceforth be safely built.[1]

The above lamentations are found in Russell's essay "A
Free Man's Worship." In this masterpiece of rhetoric, he ex-
horts us to "free" ourselves of faith in God and love for him,
for clearly, he insists, we can never hope to stand autonomously until we become unyieldingly despairful and hopeless.

Frankly, I wonder if it would behoove even a high school
sophomore to philosophize about life in so contradictory a
manner. Even a child, with a low I.Q. but with native common sense, must know that nothing good can be built on a
"firm foundation of unyielding despair." What is more, Russell
himself obviously has known his own premise to be false and
useless, for has he not lived a deeply involved and fervent life
for many years after writing these words? In 1969 he cele-
brated his ninety-seventh birthday; two years before, his auto-
biography was published. Yet, like all nihilists, he has been
strangely blind to the patent fallacy of attempting to found
the positive in the negative, of attempting to settle human
happiness on grounds that make deep joy and a conviction of
one's importance altogether impossible. With regard to happiness, the truth is actually simple: without some projection of
hope and confidence in the lasting value of his action, no person can feel any sensible cause to act at all. Russell usually
affirms this in his practical daily affairs. Otherwise, should he
not act consistently with his despairful theory and simply rid
himself completely of the nuisance of being alive?

Anyone would indeed be a tyrant if he did not honor his
neighbor's right to choose to be a nihilist. However, it is en-

tirely another matter to honor the contradictions he would foist on us as the truth about man. Is it not extremely illogical to exhort man to have great aspirations, while at the same time beseeching him to despair? All human beings have disappointments in store for them while going through life. Often we learn that we cannot possess some things which we have longed to possess. But does the fact that we have to give up some things mean that we must give up *all*? All of us have some imaginary and false needs; but also, we have many very real and essential ones. It is perfectly sensible to despair of fulfilling desires that are selfish, useless, or banal. However, any human being's reason for being alive should be to fulfill his essential needs and aspirations, and this is categorically impossible insofar as one wills to despair. All men need greater knowledge, experience, and love. No one can grow in these things except insofar as he aspires toward them and acts for them with faith and hope. Ideally, the soul of a human being should be immortal in order that he might progressively enrich the values and meanings in his identity as a person. Indeed, is this not the most crucial concept in the philosophy of autonomy—the interminable expansion and cultivation of the meaning of one's existence as a *person*? Ideally, God should exist, that we might cultivate a progressively greater love-knowledge union with him, through endless time. Russell himself admits that God *might* exist. Also he admits that we may have immortal souls. For he obviously denies that there is any absolute truth; hence, he at least indirectly allows that the value of his own negativism is "not quite beyond dispute." Considering this, is he not highly inconsistent in saying that "no philosophy which rejects" his irreligious views can ever "hope to stand"?

Seeing Russell's inconsistency, one can conclude only that his atheism is an arbitrary choice, grounded neither in factuality nor in logic. Of course, anyone has the right to make such a choice; but, by his own admission, has Russell the right to maintain it as the truth about man? That all of us are "destined to extinction," and that "the whole temple of Man's achievement must inevitably be buried beneath the debris of a universe in ruins," clearly are not objective truths revealed through established facts and reason but are only evidence of one Bertrand Russell's willful and demonic despair.

Russell has written at great length on individualism and personal integrity. I think, however, that he offers very little to a coherently rational and constructive philosophy of autonomy. He is a many-worded humanist who insists on the necessity of the individual to care responsibly for himself, but to forget about God. But in this regard he has little logic to offer. What point is there in laboriously building up ultimately to no point whatever? He tells us that he could not bear an immortal life, that indeed he would tire of living within a few decades, at most, past the span of a normal earthly life.

To me, this is indicative of a shallow care for the beauties of life and the human beings he finds in it. I cannot imagine anyone who deeply *loves* life saying that he would soon tire of living it under even the best conditions. It is easy to moralize on the subject of responsible human relations, as Russell often does. However, it is another thing entirely actually to *feel* the deep care and love which one talks about in theory. I have seen very little evidence that Russell feels much value in human personality. The truth is, the person who genuinely feels deep love for himself and others will exhibit a belief in man and his future rather than preach that he is doomed.

If Russell is convinced of the depth of his own kind of humanism, I certainly am not. If he really loves and cherishes any human being, then how can he describe him as nothing except an "accidental collocation of atoms"? This is a gross and vulgar thing to say about one's pet dog or cat, much less about a beloved friend, mate, or parent. From Russell's standpoint, a human spirit is merely a "product," a futile and absurd "accident in a backwater." Man is just an insignificant speck in a universe devoid of reason or care.

It is here that atheistic humanism betrays the shallowness and pretentiousness of its own care. For to say that a human spirit is only an accidental product is to deny that man has any *intrinsic* value as man. To begin with, the term "Chance" explains nothing when it is substituted for God. We give man a basis in rationality and purpose only by tracing his existence ultimately to some permanent Reason and Value. For in believing that a loving God exists, who can explain us and cares for us, we view man as a person of intrinsic value, as an end in himself. We view ourselves and our neighbors not as absurd and futile products but as beings grounded in eternal truth and love. Man, as a child of God, has *sui generis* importance. Every person is infinitely important. It is infinitely better for us to exist and to love one another, through God, than for us not to exist at all.

Russell must admit that he offers us nothing in substituting "Chance" for God because it is obvious that chance is not an agent endowed with essences or creative powers. Not being an agent, chance necessarily can do nothing whatever, let alone create a universe of life and love. It is therefore absurd to employ "Chance" as an agential term, as though it *were* God, and then to derive the universe and life from it. Although he presumes to have explained the origin of the world by "Chance," Russell without God really explains nothing; he simply unwittingly falls into Sartre's pit of absurdity.

A simple argument should demonstrate the arbitrary nature of atheistic humanism, which, I think, suffers from an obvious dearth of logic and true feeling for man.

There can be no doubt that there is creation in the world. We find creation taking place practically wherever we turn. Creation occurs when an agent acts on abstract possibilities to transform them into concrete realities. For example, I am an agent, and it is possible that I can build a house. Presently, the house exists only *en abstracto,* i.e., only as a possibility, for the simple reason that it has not yet been built. Of course, the parts out of which it can be built exist in the lumberyard, or in the trees in the forest, or in the primordial atomic elements which can be transformed into forests, then the trees into lumber, etc. At any rate, the house as such does not yet concretely exist. It exists only as a possibility and can never become a concrete actuality until I, or some other person, decide to *act* on the possibility of its existence. This is to say, the act of creation requires two things: (1) a possibility, and

(2) an agent who can realize the possibility and transform it into an actuality.

Obviously, there have to have always been possibilities; for if there were a time in the past when there were no possibilities, then universal impossibility is all there ever would have been. It is logically unthinkable that any possibility could ever derive from universal impossibility. Moreover, a universal state of impossibility (an infinite void in which nothing was possible) would be self-contradictory; for in such case, it would at the same time have to be possible that nothing at all was possible. This reasoning is simply *reductio ad absurdum*. Hence, that there always have existed possibilities is a logical necessity.

It is no less a logical necessity that there has always been an Agent. For it is obvious that there are agents now existing who could never have existed if there was once a time when no Agent existed.

Let me put it another way. If there was a time in the past when there was no agent, then at that time there was nothing in existence except possibilities. But this makes no sense; for obviously, if only possibilities existed, then all there ever would have been is mere possibilities. This is true simply because mere possibilities by themselves can never act. Only an *agent* can act. Therefore, there always has to have been an Agent with possibilities, or there never could have been any creative action whatever. In fact, without an Agent who could act, there could never have been any possibilities. For certainly, the term "possibility" implies that which *can* become or *can* be done. But if there were no Agent in existence, then there never could have been any possibilities, simply because nothing could ever have happened or been done.

God, the Eternal Agent with infinite possibilities, must be the creative ground of the universe, life, and man. Grounded in him, we have a foundation in abiding reason and value that can guarantee and sustain the importance of the individual human spirit throughout all time. It is precisely here, and here only, that we can discover the ultimate concept of true autonomy. I mean, any human being suffers from restricted autonomy insofar as he needlessly restricts his feeling of the *value* of himself and those around him. The more real importance a person finds in himself, the more he will act to fulfill his needs and to expand his value and meaning for himself and others. The more importance he sees in his neighbors, as ends in themselves, the more sensitively he will care for their well-being and happiness. In this act of caring, the more he will fulfill himself.

Atheistic humanism can never serve as a solid foundation for a philosophy of autonomy. As I have insisted from the beginning, no philosophy that takes man out of his context with the infinite and the eternal and reduces his importance, can do him justice. The atheist insists that man's destiny in eternity is an illusion. But this position clearly is begging the question, for it has no evidence to support it; indeed, by its own admission, it is grounded in the self-contradictory doctrine that existence is absurd. I think it should be openly admitted that this position is *negative* and is grounded in a free personal choice, not in any objective facts or reason. Of the two hypotheses (that God exists, and that he does not), certainly belief in God is the most noble and promising one for man to accept. Atheism wrongs man by tearing out from under him the only possible *lasting* basis for hope and happiness. The claim that atheism can be a foundation for genuine happiness is belied by its own obvious despairfulness and lovelessness. The man who deeply loves himself and his neighbor knows that love creates its own faith and hope, and that it will never submit to despair.

In Russell's case, the philosophy of man is limited to a barren scientism which interprets the meaning and value of life solely in terms of impersonal facts. It is as though "what science cannot discover, mankind cannot know." But in simple truth, no philosophy which excludes the *personal* facts of his life can do a human being justice; by this, I mean his needs, noble ideals, and creative aspirations toward love and beauty. Certainly, our ideal longings and aspirations are inevitably a part of human reality; indeed, they are the most meaningful and important considerations of a philosophy; and, as such, they must constitute legitimate clues to the ultimate nature of reality at large. It is incredibly naïve of the atheist to attribute all religious faith and love to escapism or ignorance. The desire to live forever arises out of love, not out of the emotional immaturity which aggressive atheists generally ascribe to religious behavior as a whole. Of course, I readily admit that the desire to live forever is grounded in wishful thinking. But then, is there anything wrong with wanting to live forever? It should be obvious that only persons who truly love life would want to live forever. Such a desire is evidence of positive love or spiritual health, not sickness. The true atheist is he who renounces eternal life on the grounds that it would not be worth living. This, I submit, is the position that is sick and in need of critical rejection. Moreover, it is also the position of real escapism; for would it not be in death, and in death only, that a person could finally escape from all life's problems, risks, pains, and efforts?

I would readily agree that the orthodox conception of heaven (where persons have no efforts to exert, no problems to solve, and no challenges to accept) is essentially escapist in nature. Such lethally beatific conditions would bore to distraction the person who possesses a true spirit of living. In such bliss, one scarcely would be *living* at all. However, this notion of heaven, as an insipid ecstasy, must be rejected along with atheism on the basis that both represent a wish to escape from life. The person who wholeheartedly affirms life will allow nothing to reduce needlessly his possibilities for living, either now or in the future. He knows that the purpose of life is simply more living; and, if there is any reason why he should not continue this adventure forever, then for the same reason he should not live for another minute. If the existence of a human spirit is intrinsically valuable, then our importance is established for eternity. If we settle for anything less than intrinsic importance, we do ourselves an infinite injustice. The desire to live forever is no more irrational or selfish than the desire to live for another hour: altogether the contrary, the absence of this desire is only evidence of a deflated spirit, which can provide no support for a lasting and successful self-concept for man.

Neither theism nor atheism can be proved with conclusive evidence of an absolute nature. But one thing is certain: to take either position requires faith; and atheistic faith is stupid because it needlessly acts against man and his future possibilities. Atheism acts against our most promising hypotheses and best interests. It unquestionably is in our best interest that God exists and loves us. It would be infinitely better for him to exist than not to exist, and we need him whether we admit it or not. It uplifts us to love him, to seek the fulfillment and adventure of an immortal life that is grounded in him. The affirmation of God requires faith, simply because our understanding of the Infinite can never be complete. Indeed, how could a finite mind ever fully encompass the Infinite, and lose its curiosity and wonder? By virtue of its very terms, the Infinite can never be encompassed, and it is precisely for this reason that we have permanent promise in a future of endless possibilities.

Atheism places its faith ultimately in nothingness or in death. According to this woeful philosophy, all spirits eventually will be destroyed, and in their death all purpose, value, and meaning will be lost. In death, there can be no autonomy whatever, simply because the living agent is reduced to nothingness for eternity.

In contrast to this negative faith, religious faith is positive. It is founded in a positive assessment of the nature and value of the human spirit and its future possibilities. In this faith and love, we shall never flinch. No moment of our lives must be allowed ever to lose its meaning.

But of course, the nihilists have their retort to this. Such talk, they say, is nothing more than useless self-deception and dumb sentiment. But I would ask a very plain and simple question here. What have they to offer us in the place of our faith? What do they give to man that is as constructive and fulfilling as the love for God which they know nothing of or else reject because of its demands? How can they *prove* their negative premises, which they claim constitute the objective truth? What argument has Camus that a human being can accept hopelessness and death, yet be truly happy? What persuasion has Sartre that the alternatives to religious faith and love (i.e., desperation and despair) are more realistic and manly? Man must have faith in himself, Erich Fromm insists; but I ask him: What is *wrong* with the kind of religious faith and love that have most enhanced my joy in living? What value has Russell's "unyielding despair" when we can have unyielding faith and hope instead?

According to Sartre, everything comes from nothing and is absurd. But how can this be an argument against God? For if a human spirit, a sunset, and a universe can come from nothing, then there is no reason why God could not also come from nothing. This certainly would be no less absurd. I say to Sartre, *front à front:* The obstacle to your faith in God is not objective evidence or logic (your nihilism has ruled out these things as impossible); consequently, is it not simply your personal will? Is it not true that you *will* not to believe? Do you not *prefer* atheism, simply because if God existed he would have a claim on your soul and your "absolute freedom" would topple as a myth?

According to Russell, all has come out of "Chance." This is so sheer an evasion of evidence and logic that it is totally senseless. If atheism is to be supported at all, it must be on the human *will*; the doctrine cannot rest on chance. If this simple word ("Chance") could create the infinitely complex world we live in and know—an absurd idea—then there is no reason why it could not also create God, for this would be no less absurd. Logically, the only thing derivable from nothing is nothing. The nihilists themselves grant this, and on this basis attempt to establish that all existence is absurd. Since the absurdity of existence is their fundamental dogma, is it not impossible for them to argue *logically* against God? If a grain of sand can come out of nothing for a moment, which is absurd, then is there any reason why God could not have come out of nothing for eternity?

Within the framework of Sartre's and Russell's metaphysics, if anything at all can exist, then certainly God can exist, and there can be a destiny in eternity for all of those who love him. That the Lord exists, and that in his love and power we have eternal promise—this is a possibility that can never be refuted. Just this possibility is all that the autonomous man will ever need in order to take action for a greater good.

According to Russell, we should logically reject God because of his "omnipotence." An omnipotent God would never have created a world plagued with the ugliness and misery that we find in this life. If God really existed, he would have created a perfect world, or at least one in which human beings would not be subject to evils and suffering.

It is unfortunate that Russell has ignored other philosophies of God (such as those of Brightman, Berdyaev, and Hartshorne). In the new theology, the Lord is worshiped for his intrinsically good will and perfect love, but is acknowledged to be limited in his power. From the assumption that God is a creative Person, with infinite possibilities in his future, it does not follow that he possesses *absolute* power; indeed the contrary, absolute power would entail the simultaneous actualization of all possibilities, or the complete fulfillment *at once* of all ideals. But if this were the case with God (as it is erroneously considered to be in traditional theology), then he could not be a creative Person with any future or adventure before him. For if all possibilities of creative action already were fulfilled in God, there could be no possibilities for action since all possibilities would have been already transformed into actualities. It is very contradictory to say that God is infinitely creative and that he has absolute power. For in order to have an eternal future grounded in infinite possibilities, it must be impossible for God to fulfill all of his possibilities at once—indeed ever. If the creative possibilities in him are infinite, then there is indeed no end to them; and, since he acts on them without absolute power, the process of life must go on forever.

The answer to Russell's argument against God is simple. We must do away with that contradictory and useless conception of him as the cosmic Mighty Mouse of passé theology. The real Lord is a cosmic Person, caught up joyfully and willfully in the creative struggle that is essential to the existence of any person. Because God is rational and moral and loves us, he grants his children freedom of choice, without which we could never know self-esteem, responsibility, and dignity. And because he allows us this freedom, he makes himself subject to the suffering we cause him when we choose to act in evil ways. Since his power is not absolute, he is limited in his control of possible and real evils in the same world which makes freedom, love, and dignity possible. Is it not obvious, from the facts of the world we live in, that the Lord is *limited* in his power to prevent misfortune and suffering? What we must not lose sight of is the fact that he himself suffers because of the generosity of his love. It is his love that makes him amenable to the effects of our own actions when they are evil. And because he is a Person and a Father, we add to his joy through our acts of positive faith and love for him. Our faith is not in Aristotle's omnipotent Unmoved Mover. Such a deity would be an empty abstraction, an unhistorical and impersonal being unaffected by man. The God of the Cross is a Person who sees infinite value in each of his children. We do not worship him because he has absolute power. Such power would not be intrinsically deserving of worship even if God had it. What matters is how he uses his power in his loving care for his creatures. Our faith is in a good God, not an absolutely powerful one. God should be worshiped because of his benevolence and the price that he has to pay for being God. And by this, I mean his willingness to suffer in behalf of creative freedom and responsible love for his children.

Traditionally, theologians have attributed to the Lord an *absolutely complete knowledge* of the future. According to the classical view of his omniscience, God knows everything that is going to happen in the future because, in reality, he is timeless eternity in which the past, present, and future inhere in an absolutely immutable now. In effect, this is saying that God is history complete, for everything that could ever possibly happen has already happened; consequently, the future is already determined. In fact, there is no future at all—it is merely an illusion of the finite mind—for in God the past, present, and future always have been, are now, and always will be the same. God is eternity. Time is an illusion, and God is absolutely complete. He is absolutely changeless, and absolutely happy or self-fulfilled. Also, he is omnipresent being, meaning, he is all-inclusive being. There is nothing in existence that is not a part of his domain of order or being. He is the Whole, and he is perfectly complete. In him, all possibilities always have been, are now, and always will be perfectly fulfilled.

In other words, there really are no possibilities, and there never have been. Our minds deceive us when we think we perceive such things in the world as change, incompletion, loneliness, suffering, evil, freedom, purpose, and a future of as-yet-unfulfilled *real possibilities*. This is to say, all that could ever possibly happen has already happened. In fact, since God is immutable, history is an illusion and nothing has ever really happened at all. Indeed, how could it in an absolutely self-fulfilled, eternally changeless God? From the standpoint of classical theism, there is not now, never has been, and never will be any real possibility.

Contrary to what most ministers think, this absurd doctrine of God as a cosmic *fixation* is nowhere to be found in the teachings of either the Old Testament or the New. Rather, it has come largely out of the metaphysics of Aristotle and the broodings of his famous academic disciple, Thomas Aquinas. The teachings of Jesus are clearly so inconsonant with those of Aristotle, I find it incredible that the church would have fostered a theological fantasy that theoretically has shorn God of his creative purposefulness and heroic involvement in history. A fixated, immutable being could never be a creative Father. God could not be absolutely changeless and at the same time be a Person with creative possibilities in a real future. The very act of creation brings into existence something which previously did not exist in God's domain of order, except as a possibility grounded in the primordial essences. Creation results in a *change* in the world; it brings in something *new*.

What is most objectionable in traditional theology is its theoretical undermining of the possibility of autonomy. Aristotle's God could never create any children at all, let alone allow them personal autonomy in freedom of choice. If the future is already totally determined, which it would have to be before God could have an infallible knowledge of it, then the freedom of man to choose (and thus partially determine himself and his destiny) is a pointless illusion. If the future is totally determined already, then obviously there is nothing any of us can do to alter or deter it in any way. If there is no real distinction between the past, present, and future in the immutable God, then there is no future at all—indeed, there is not even a real past; there is only an eternally changeless now.

We need to rid theology of this archaic conception of God, for it would reduce the Lord to an extravaganza of useless and obtuse contradictions.

God knows all the logical possibilities of the future, since logical possibilities have to have existed always in order to exist at all. If something were logically impossible, not even God could ever make it possible, if we are to deem him a logical God. Logical possibilities are primordial and eternal; they were never created by God but simply have existed always as an inherent part of his essential being. Also, he knows all things that will *necessarily* happen in the future because of the laws of nature which, through his action, will inevitably bring them to pass. However, there remains the ever-present fact of man's freedom of choice, which God has endowed us with and intends for us to employ. Logically, God knows all the alternative possibilities between which we might choose in the future. But because of our freedom of choice and considerable power for self-determination, he cannot tell in advance what choices we shall make. Obviously, he cannot know our future choices because they have not yet been made. If all our future actions were known by God (that is, already determined), then plainly we could have no real choice in the matter. To be free at all, a choice must be between alternative possibilities for *action not heretofore determined*. This means not determined by God or any other power.

Of course, the alternative possibilities for action are limited in number for any human being at any given time. The ultimate structure or scope of our possibilities is grounded in the fundamental, essential nature of God. But in the open future, this scope reaches out literally to no end and thus holds a promise for the Lord and his children that fills the autonomous person with an unquenchable spiritual fire.

A human being can be only as autonomous as how many possibilities he has, and how faithfully and vitally he chooses to act upon them. The act of despair is a closing out of possibilities. The more despairful one is, the more he has narrowed down his vision and awareness of the possibilities before him in the future; hence, the more he has diminished his power to act upon them to fulfill his life.

I shall conclude with a summary statement of my philosophical position in this book. To study man properly, we must regard him as:

1. *A spiritual agent* of intrinsic value, who cannot be reduced to an accident, a product, an absurdity, or a futility.
2. *A free agent,* who is responsible for his actions whenever it is possible for him to choose.
3. *A self-transcending agent,* whose growth in self-significance and self-value requires a future of unlimited possibilities.
4. *An intelligible agent,* whose being is grounded in a cosmic order structured in permanent reason and love.

In short, I equate the spiritual autonomy of a man with his *value.* We are only as autonomous as how much value we discover in the world, in ourselves, and in God.

Addendum:
Additional Displeasure

IN PRESENTING my own position, I must acknowledge having taken a certain license in my use of the word "realism." Like any other school, "realism" is divided by a host of deviant viewpoints on such vital questions as the nature of the mind, the self, and the world. Indeed, this is so much the case that it is often difficult to find much common ground between "critical realists," "neorealists," "scientific realists," "personal realists," etc. Some views classified under this general school are so reductionistic that I should accuse them of dissolving the individual just as much as do those of the out-and-out nihilists. In fact, some "realists' " views on the nature of the self are basically so relativistic, or behavioristic, that they are as inimical to autonomy as pragmatism or existentialism. For example, Bertrand Russell often is classified as a realist even though he calls himself a "logical atomist." Yet, his views on the self are as diverse from mine as are Dewey's and Sartre's. However, I have had no intention of bogging down in a hopeless and useless argument over the proper use of philosophical terms. It seems to me that what really matters is that one try to present his position as clearly and consistently as possible, for labels are not of any great importance.

Although both Dewey and Camus are dead, their philosophical influence is now greater than ever, and this is why I have referred to them as though they were living today.

I regret that preoccupation with other matters makes a more exhaustive analysis of nihilism impossible at this time.

The history of philosophy is replete with famed thinkers whose metaphysical and psychological systems theorize the individual into essentially nothing. For example, C. H. Cooley argues that

the individual is not *separable* from the human *whole;* men are literally one body. . . . A separate individual is an *abstraction* unknown to experience (i.e., not knowable at all). . . . All is alike cause and effect; there is no logical primacy, no *independent variable*. . . . Mind is all one growth, and we cannot draw any distinct line between personal thought and other thought. . . . Self and others *do not exist as mutually exclusive social facts.*[1]

Like Dewey, Cooley obviously reduces the mind to a theory of internal relations; in effect, he completely denies the possibility of individual agents who can function autonomously even to the slightest degree.

I have already criticized Dewey's reasoning that would theoretically undermine the person as an agent. But here, I should like to quote him further. Speaking of the conditions necessary for thought, he tells us that "concrete habits do all the perceiving, recognizing, imagining, recalling, judging, conceiving and reasoning that is done," and that "the scientific man and the philosopher like the carpenter, the physician and politician, *know* with their *habits* not with their 'consciousness.' "[2] Obviously, there is no room in Dewey's system for autonomy, for the simple reason that a human being is not a freely functioning entity but only a bundle of impersonally conditioned habits. Frankly, it tries my patience that so esteemed a philosopher would reduce all of us to nothing except "habits." How can a habit "judge," "reason," and "conceive"? In Dewey's system, a human being has no mind, no freedom of choice, no real capacity for self-determination. In short, there is no such thing as a *person*. This ridiculous position has been made famous also in the behavioristic psychologies of Watson, Skinner, Freud, and many others.

Dewey was influenced enormously by Hegel. In this German philosopher we find the doctrine of internal relations developed to the point of erasing all existential entities or identities. Regarding the existence of really separate or individual realities, there are neither subjects nor objects, nor any other kind of concrete entities. The separate parts and the whole are mutually constituted and determined and in no way really distinguishable from each other. This is due to the utter interfusion and mutual conditioning of all things (as though, under such circumstances, the term "things" could still have a meaning!). According to Hegel, "there is nothing in the effect which is not in the cause, and the cause is cause only in the effect. . . . Insofar as the effect returns to the cause, it is itself cause."[3]

In Hegelian philosophy, "the individual exists only in social manifestations and expression. *The individual apart from other individuals is meaningless.* . . . Each individual finds his being *in all others* and exists in perfect unity with them."[4] In essence, Hegel reduces the universe to a *static* whole, in which distinctions between past, present, and future are impossible, just as any logical distinction between parts as existential entities is also impossible. For since all causes and effects interfuse into One Absolute Being, any distinction between one individual and another, or between separate events in time, becomes simply an illusional abstraction. According to Hegel, we do not have individual minds with which we produce our own thoughts. Rather, there is only one mind, that of the One Absolute Being. That each of us is a separate agent largely responsible for his own thoughts is ultimately an illusion. Our thoughts are not thought by us, but rather by the Universal Mind.

A similar dissolution of the person as an agent is found in the thinking of Bernard Bosanquet. This famous philosopher tells us: "Mind and society are really the *same* fabric regarded from different points of view. What outwardly are social groups are inwardly mental systems. . . . The finite self has no *being* apart from its membership of the whole. . . . Behind the finite mind there is the driving power of the whole with which it is *continuous.*"[5] This means that "a synthesis of different personalities actually takes place. Common language *admits one self in different bodies,* and the general will seems to be an indisputable fact."[6]

Like Cooley, Hegel, and Dewey, Bosanquet destroys the individual's identity by decomposing him into the whole. In this radical relativism, persons cannot be really related because they cannot exist as real terms between which real relations can occur. Certainly, if there are no separate minds, then there are no distinct agents between which, or in which, any relations can take place. How, indeed, can one self be in different bodies? Bosanquet obviously equates language with thought; this means that if Harry and John speak the same language, they have the same soul in their different bodies. Is this not a bit ridiculous? Is there a self in a dictionary simply because it is filled with words? Are John and Harry one person at the moment they simultaneously say "hello" to each other? How could they greet each other as separate persons if they were one and the same? Like all relativists, Bosanquet refuses any distinction between thought and the thinker; that is, if ten people are thinking the same thought, then there is only one thinker. According to the relativist, "the self is in an internal relationship not only with other selves but also with nature. There is no absolute (clear) distinction between the individual and his environment; the self is the inwardness of the environment itself. You cannot say where self ends and environment begins."[7]

How curious this is: the world's most renowned philosophers so devoted to abolishing all meaningful distinctions between one thing and another. Note the ease with which Josiah Royce reduces real individuals to a fuzzy, cosmic soup: "The unity of selfhood includes all individuals; it is the Absolute, the Self of Selves, the eternal All-Knower. Our fragmentary lives are fragments of this eternally *whole* and *complete* life."[8] This means that, in God, all reality is fixed, static, and finished. The only reality is the Absolute Mind. Our finite, human minds are but timeless thoughts or abstractions in the mind of God. Exactly like Hegel, Royce completely melts the individual into his "social relations." He declares that "self-conscious functions are *all* of them, in their finite, human, and primary aspect, *social* functions, due to the habit of human intercourse."[9]

As a real individual, must I not have a "unity" of my own, that is within myself? Can I have nothing at all within me that is private, unique, not socially determined or possessed by those around me? Have I no facets, traits, thoughts, or feelings that have been determined uniquely and solely by myself? How can I sustain my own unity of selfhood if, as Royce says, my self must "include all individuals"?

Within the framework of Roycean metaphysics, there certainly can never be any agent who *acts* for any purpose at all. Indeed, how can action be possible if both time and the agent are illusions of the "finite mind"? It is even more puzzling that there can be finite minds at all if the assumption is correct that there is really only one mind and it is infinite. After the manner of all relativists, Royce reduces the evolutionary process of life to a mere semantical illusion. For if all causes and effects interfuse to make one, which means that history is already complete in eternity, then indeed, both time and the finite mind are meaningless terms. We have here a perfect example of the traditional theologian, who would describe God as creative and active yet reduce him in effect to an illogical and static phantom. Royce tells us that "a man becomes self-conscious only in the most intimate connection with the growth of his social consciousness. These two forms of consciousness are not *separable*."[10]

Not separable? How can there be relations between truly different or distinct individuals if "their forms of consciousness are not separable" one from the other? How can we speak rationally of relations between selves in the plural if, in reality, there is only one self?

Royce converts the individual into only an abstract attribute of society, then makes a society impossible. How can there exist either an individual or a group of individuals if there is no agent capable of functioning in some way as an independent variable? In the metaphysics of relativism, there are no such things as independent variables, simply because no one can exist, think, or function in any way independently of others.

Cooley, for example, tells us that "the growth of the individual mind is not a *separate* growth, but rather a differentiation within the general mind."[11] Thinking along this same line, J. S. Mackenzie (early-century sociologist) insists:

We are members of one another. . . . .Man does not at first naturally think of himself as an independent individual, but rather as a part of a system; and this system may in a very real sense be called a "self," since it is the universe to which the individual refers his life. . . . .Every individual belongs to a social system. An isolated individual is even inconceivable. The *I* or idealized self is not realized in any *one* individual, but finds its realization rather in the *relations* of persons to one another.[12]

Thus, a human being is neither an agent nor any other type of real entity. On the contrary, he is constituted solely of his relations; he is actually neither this nor that, since his relations are without terms and lost in an indefinite "whole." Earlier, I pointed out that relations without real terms are both logically and existentially meaningless, a point that Mackenzie and his more recent followers seem curiously incapable of understanding. He too insists that "the individual apart from society is an abstraction."[13]

Considering the more up-to-date thinkers, I should include both Alfred North Whitehead and Charles Hartshorne among those who deny the reality of the agent. Undoubtedly, both of these philosophers are as highly esteemed as any of our time, at least in academic circles. Yet, both reduce the *I* to nothing except an empty object of mentation. Once in a conversation with Hartshorne, I insisted that "I am an *agent*," only to hear him reply: "That term is a mere abstraction!" Hartshorne and Whitehead treat the mind not as an agent but rather as a "series of events," "occasions," or "acts." How very curious that these philosophers place so great an emphasis on freedom, responsibility, and individual integrity. My problem with them is this: If a human individual is not an agent, then to whom can responsibility be assigned? If there is no agent, then by whom can choices be made? Is it not meaningless to assign responsibility to mere past "events," "occasions," or "acts"? Do acts commit themselves? Do motives create themselves?

Do thoughts think themselves? Do decisions decide themselves, and choices choose themselves? In his *Logic of Perfection,* Hartshorne rejects the enduring agent as a mere fiction. Says he: "The real agent is always momentary," and "The abiding ever-identical agent is an abstraction."[14] Given to using the term in quotes, he rejects the "soul" as a myth.

Hartshorne and Whitehead allow no logical distinction between the predicate and the subject, between action and the actor. Their psychology of mind terminates in a mere phenomenology—a view of the human spirit as only a "set of relations" or a "stream of events." Frankly, I see no difference in this respect between Sartre's deduction of mental conduct from nothing and Hartshorne's and Whitehead's deduction of it from a cosmic order that has no agents.

I should admit that a human spirit is indeed a very mysterious being. How the spirit can *exist* or *be,* and at the same time determine the *becoming* of its own expanding identity, is impossible for the human mind to explain. We might as well accept this certain fact: the human mind can experience both being and becoming but can explain neither. But the fact that we cannot explain this commonsense knowledge is no ground on which to reject it as unreal. The assumption that we can experience or know only that which we can exhaustively explain or understand is incredibly naïve.

It is characteristic of "process philosophers" to subordinate being to becoming, or else ambiguously to equate them as one. For an intelligible interpretation of reality, we need all three concepts: being, becoming, and unbecoming. The nouns and adjectives of our language refer to essences, qualities, and subjects and objects that *are.* And except for the verb "to be," all verbs refer to a *process,* i.e., to something that is becoming or unbecoming. We abuse the laws of language logic when we throw out nouns and adjectives, as though they never refer to any definite *beings* in reality. If we reduce the human spirit to only a series of acts, once again we just end up with relations between relations, which is preposterously ambiguous. If *I* am only an abstraction, it follows that I am only an object or a product, no less than a stone. Now I should ask: When an abstraction is being made, who is doing the abstracting? Process philosophers allow no logical distinction between the abstraction itself (the object of mental action), the act of abstracting (a process), and the actor who does the abstracting (the responsible agent or subject). Certainly, an abstraction is not a subject; it is the object of the subject's thought.

To sustain his autonomy, the individual must surrender in no way to the charge that he is "only an abstraction," only "a set of relations," or only "a series of events." The "process philosophers" speak to us of "integrity" and "unity" in the individual's personality and character. But I ask, How can anyone be responsible for unifying himself if he does not exist as the agent who can do the unifying?

That a person is only a series of acts is a useless and degrading assumption, and is itself only an abstraction.

True autonomy requires that we honor the reality of every *I*. Personal pronouns are not empty abstractions without reference to real agents. There is no language (nor is one possible) in which human beings can communicate intelligibly with one another without using pronouns. If personal pronouns do not refer to real agents, then they refer to nothing meaningful at all. What would the reader think if I said to him: "You are nothing but an abstraction"!

Plainly, when there is an abstraction in my thinking, it is because *I* am producing the abstraction; an abstraction cannot act. Only an agent can act. Consequently, why torture commonsense wisdom by assigning responsibility for action to a mere abstraction? I do not, and cannot, understand entirely *what* I am, or exactly the possibilities of *how* I am, or all the reasons *why* I am. Nonetheless, I know unmistakably *that* I am, and that I am largely responsible for my acts.

There is a terrible danger in reducing the human spirit to a mere abstraction. So many evils have come out of this nonsense that I shudder in pondering the fact that philosophers are doing it more and more.

Appendix:
Omniscience Versus
Freedom

IN CLEARING UP the mess of classical theism, some added notes might be of service here. Traditionally, theologians have said that *God is absolutely omniscient.* As I mentioned earlier, this means that God is eternity complete. That is, in God history is complete. God is timeless eternity in which all our time distinctions (the past, present, and future) inhere in an absolutely immutable *now.* In effect, this is saying that in God the past, present, and future are the same because God is the perfect and completed Whole. Also, it is saying that in reality there is no change or time. If we could see reality as God sees it, we would see that nothing is really happening, and that the process of ongoing history is an illusion in our finite minds. Elaborate arguments for this position are found in the writings of Josiah Royce, Borden Parker Bowne, Bernard Bosanquet, the Scholastics, and innumerable others.

The assumption of God's absolute omniscience means that he already knows everything that can ever possibly be known about the "future," since the whole of reality is already fully determined, fully included in his present being and knowledge. However, the classical theist is equally as insistent in his belief that *man has freedom of the will to choose between alternative possibilities for action and has a capacity to determine freely, to a certain extent, what the future will be.*

It appears to me that the contradiction between these two assumptions should be obvious to anyone who approaches the matter logically, with a mind free from the emotional bind of strong theological conditioning. Briefly, my critique of the contradiction can be presented in these simple steps:

1. Yesterday John Doe murdered his wife with a gun.
2. God has always known, with infallible certainty, precisely how this event would happen and precisely at what time.
3. Therefore, the event could not fail to happen; for otherwise, its failing to happen would disprove the infallibility of God's knowledge of the future.
4. Clearly, John's murdering his wife was inevitable, i.e., was certain to happen, or else it could not be known in advance with certainty and could not be predicted by God.
5. Since the murder could not fail to happen, it is absurd to say that John had it within his power, or was free, to prevent it from happening.
6. It is a contradiction in terms to say that the murder has always been a known fact in God's mind (an eternally foregone historical fact), and at the same time say that it might never have occurred at all.

The traditionalist has a pat answer to this, namely, that "God simply has always known how we will choose because his knowledge is infinite."

Notice that he speaks of how we *will* choose, even after denying that the future tense can have any real meaning since it is only an illusion in our mistaken minds. In simple truth, if the future is already absolutely fixed, there is nothing any one of us can do to change it one whit. Consequently, the idea of alternative possibilities for action (freedom) must be a myth.

Logically, we must either give up the idea that God is totally omniscient or drop the notion of freedom. Certainly, we can never give up the idea of freedom without sacrificing the sense of moral responsibility that accompanies the sense of choice. And this we cannot afford to be without. But there is no loss whatever in relinquishing a static god and turning to the Lord who loves us and needs us and faces the open future with us.

Notes

CHAPTER ONE

1. Sidney Hook, *The Quest for Being* (New York: Dell Publishing Co., 1961), p. 159. Italics his.

2. Justus Buchler (ed.), *The Philosophy of Peirce: Selected Writings* (New York: Harcourt, Brace & World, 1940; London: Routledge and Kegan Paul, 1940), pp. 46-47, 54. Italics mine. Used by permission of Routledge and Dover Publications, New York.

3. Frederick C. Neff, "Pragmatism and Education," in PHILOSOPHY OF EDUCATION: Essays and Commentaries, edited by Hobert C. Burns and Charles J. Brauner. Copyright © 1962 The Ronald Press Company, New York, p. 313. Quotations from this book are used by permission.

4. John Dewey, *Reconstruction in Philosophy* (Boston: Beacon Press, 1948), p. 135. Quotations from this book are used by permission.

5. Dewey, *Essays in Experimental Logic* (Chicago: University of Chicago Press, 1916), p. 331.

CHAPTER TWO

1. Neff, *op. cit.,* p. 309.

2. Donald Arnstine, *Philosophy of Education: Learning and Schooling* (New York: Harper & Row, 1967), pp. 103, 104, 105. The following quotations have been arranged for convenience of interpretation of author's points. Quotations from this book are used by permission.

3. *Ibid.,* p. 109.

4. *Ibid.,* p. 106. Italics mine, except in first sentence.

5. *Ibid.*, p. 110. Italics mine.

6. *Ibid.*, p. 106. Italics mine.

7. *Ibid.* Italics mine.

8. *Ibid.* Italics mine.

9. *Ibid.*, p. 102.

10. Dewey in *Experience and Nature, The Knower and the Known, Human Nature and Conduct, Logic: The Theory of Inquiry,* and other works.

11. Neff, *op. cit.,* p. 319.

12. Dewey, *Experience and Nature* (Chicago: Open Court Publishing Co., 1925), p. 232. Subsequent quotations are from this edition unless otherwise noted. Used by permission.

13. *Ibid.*, p. 231. Italics mine.

14. Lawrence G. Thomas, "The Ontology of Experimentalism," *Educational Theory,* VI (July, 1956), 177-83. Italics mine in first sentence. Quotations from this article are used by permission.

15. *Ibid.* Italics mine.

16. *Ibid.* Italics mine.

CHAPTER THREE

1. My numbering of the principles of pragmatism is for convenience only.

2. Viktor Frankl, *Man's Search for Meaning: An Introduction to Logotherapy* (New York: Washington Square Press, Copyright, © 1959, 1963 by Viktor E. Frankl), pp. 205-7. Italics mine, except in third sentence. Reprinted by permission of Simon & Schuster, Inc.

3. Jean-Paul Sartre, *Existentialism,* trans. Bernard Frechtman (New York: Philosophical Library, 1947), p. 18. Italics mine. Quotations from this book are used by permission of Philosophical Library and Methuen & Co., Ltd., London, the British publishers. (British title: *Existentialism and Humanism.*)

4. Sartre, *The Transcendence of the Ego,* trans. Forrest Williams

and Robert Kirkpatrick (New York: Noonday Press [Farrar, Straus & Giroux], 1957), pp. 98-99. Used by permission.

5. Friedrich Nietzsche, *Beyond Good and Evil*, Gateway Ed. trans. and with an intro. by Marianne Cowan (Chicago: Henry Regnery Co., 1955), p. 18.

6. Sartre, *Nausea* (London: Purnell and Sons, Ltd., 1949), p. 151. Quotations from this book are used by permission of Editions Gallimard, publisher of original French edition, and New Directions, owner of U.S. rights.

7. *Ibid.*, p. 180.

8. *Ibid.*, p. 176. Parenthesis and italic word "absolute" mine.

9. Thomas, *op. cit.*

CHAPTER FOUR

1. Arnstine, *op. cit.*, pp. 109, 105, 107. Quotes have been arranged for convenience of interpretation of author's view. Italics and parenthesis mine.

2. Dewey, *Experience and Nature*, p. 231. Italics mine.

3. *Ibid.*, pp. 231-32.

4. Dewey, *Experience and Nature* (paperback ed.; New York: Dover Publications, Inc., 1958), p. 8.

5. Thomas, *op. cit.*

6. Neff, *op. cit.*, p. 305. Italics mine.

7. Dewey, *Philosophy and Civilization* (New York: G. P. Putnam's Sons, 1931), p. 24. Parenthesis and italics mine.

8. *Ibid.*

9. Neff, *op. cit.*, p. 304. Italics mine.

10. *Ibid.* Italics mine.

11. Thomas, *op. cit.* Italics mine.

12. *Ibid.* Italics mine.

13. Dewey, *Experience and Nature*, p. 3a.

14. *Ibid.*, p. 232.

15. *Ibid.* (paperback ed. previously cited), p. 8.

16. Neff, *op. cit.,* p. 311.

17. *Ibid.* Italics mine.

18. *Ibid.,* p. 319. Italics mine.

19. *Ibid.,* p. 310.

20. *Ibid.*

21. *Ibid.,* p. 311.

22. *Ibid.*

23. John Herman Randall, Jr., and Justus Buchler, *Philosophy: An Introduction* (New York: Barnes and Noble, 1942), p. 142. Italics mine.

24. Neff, *op. cit.,* p. 310.

25. *Ibid.,* pp. 308-9. Italics mine. Sentences rearranged for convenience of quoting.

26. Dewey, *Creative Intelligence* (New York: Henry Holt and Company, 1917), p. 55.

CHAPTER FIVE

1. Bertrand Russell, *Philosophy* (New York: W. W. Norton & Company, 1927), p. 235. Quotations from this book are used by permission of the British publisher, George Allen & Unwin, Ltd., London.

2. *Ibid.,* p. 233. Parenthesis mine.

3. *Ibid.* Italics mine.

4. *Ibid.,* p. 225.

5. Russell, *Religion and Science* (London: Butterworth, 1935), pp. 175, 176, 230-31, 235-36, 238-39. Used by permission of the Clarendon Press, Oxford.

6. Russell, *Philosophy,* p. 233.

7. *Ibid.,* pp. 226, 233, 234. Italics mine in word "desired."

8. Earl Cunningham, "First Principles for a Modern Philosophy of Education," *Educational Theory* (January, 1955), pp. 1-12. Used by permission.

9. *Ibid.,* p. 28.

10. If I recall correctly, this phrase, or a similar one, was used by W. H. Whyte in *The Organization Man.*

11. Neff, *op. cit.,* p. 304.

12. *Ibid.,* p. 310.

13. Randall and Buchler, *op. cit.,* p. 124.

14. Neff, *op. cit.,* p. 308.

15. Dewey, *Logic: The Theory of Inquiry* (New York: Henry Holt and Company, 1938), p. 461.

16. *Ibid.,* p. 456.

17. Neff, *op. cit.,* p. 308.

18. *Ibid.*

19. This quote is directly from Dewey, not James: *Reconstruction in Philosophy,* p. 156.

20. William James, *Pragmatism* (New York: Longmans, Green & Co., 1907), pp. 45-46.

21. Neff, *op. cit.,* p. 307.

22. *Ibid.,* p. 315.

23. *Ibid.,* p. 310.

24. Dewey and James Tufts, *Ethics* (rev. ed.; New York: Henry Holt and Company, 1932), p. 173.

25. Dewey, *Reconstruction in Philosophy,* p. 170. Italics mine.

26. Dewey, *Experience and Nature,* p. 425.

27. Dewey, *Human Nature and Conduct* (New York: Modern Library, 1930), p. 239. Italics mine. Quotations from this book are used by permission of Holt, Rinehart and Winston, copyright owner and publisher of original edition.

28. Charles Frankel, *The Case for Modern Man* (New York: Harper & Row, 1955), p. 135. Italics mine. Quotations from this book are used by permission.

29. *Ibid.,* p. 197. Italics mine.

30. Frankel, *The Love of Anxiety and Other Essays* (New York: Harper & Row, 1951), pp. 138-41. Italics mine, except word "Weltanschauung." Quotations from this book are used by permission.

31. *Ibid.,* p. 141. Italics mine.

32. *Ibid.,* p. 143. Italics mine.

33. *Ibid.,* p. 144. Italics mine.

CHAPTER SIX

1. William K. Frankena, *Ethics,* © 1963, p. 46. Italics mine. By permission of Prentice-Hall, Inc.

2. I am not familiar with the Greek rendering; this obviously is the famous Latin translation.

3. Dietrich Bonhoeffer, *Ethics,* ed. Eberhard Bethge, trans. Neville Horton Smith (New York: The Macmillan Co., 1955).

CHAPTER SEVEN

1. Albert Camus, *Le Mythe de Sisyphe* (Paris: Librairie Gallimard, 1942), p. 75.

2. Camus, *Les Temps Modernes,* August, 1952. Italics mine.

3. *Ibid.* Italics mine.

CHAPTER EIGHT

1. Matthew 7:1-2.

CHAPTER ELEVEN

1. Erich Fromm, *The Art of Loving* (New York: Harper & Row, 1956).

2. Camus, *Lettres à un ami allemand* (Paris: Librairie Gallimard, 1948), pp. 78-79. My translation and italics.

3. Sartre, *Being and Nothingness*, trans. and with an intro. by Hazel E. Barnes (New York: Philosophical Library, 1956), p. 615.

4. Sartre, *Existentialism*, p. 60.

5. *Ibid.*, pp. 37-38.

6. *Ibid.*, pp. 26, 27. Italics mine, except term "a priori."

7. *Ibid.*, p. 58. Italics mine, except term "a priori."

8. *Ibid.*, p. 24. Italics mine.

9. *Ibid.*, p. 18. Italics mine.

10. Sartre, *Being and Nothingness*, p. 615.

11. Sartre, *Existentialism*, p. 53.

12. Sartre, *Nausea*, p. 176. Italics mine.

CHAPTER TWELVE

1. Russell, "A Free Man's Worship," *Mysticism and Logic* (New York: W. W. Norton & Company, 1929), pp. 47-48. Used by permission of the British publisher, George Allen & Unwin, Ltd., London.

ADDENDUM

1. C. J. Bittner, *The Development of the Concept of the Social Nature of the Self* (Iowa City: Fred Hahne Co. [privately printed], 1932), p. 321. Italics mine. (Originally, a Ph.D. diss., University of Iowa, 1932.)

2. Dewey, *Human Nature and Conduct*, pp. 177, 182. Italics mine.

3. Bittner, *op. cit.*, p. 321.

4. *Ibid.*, p. 351. Italics mine. (This is part of C. J. Bittner's summary of Hegel's position.)

5. *Ibid.*, p. 321. Italics mine.

6. *Ibid.* Italics mine.

7. *Ibid.,* pp. 320-21. Parenthesis mine.

8. *Ibid.,* p. 321. Italics mine.

9. *Ibid.,* p. 322. Italics mine.

10. *Ibid.,* p. 321. Italics mine.

11. *Ibid.,* p. 305. Italics mine.

12. *Ibid.,* pp. 303-5. Italics mine.

13. *Ibid.,* p. 321.

14. Charles Hartshorne, *The Logic of Perfection* (LaSalle, Illinois: Open Court Publishing Co., 1962), p. 201.